MAKING BOOKS
Across the Curriculum

By Natalie Walsh

S C H O L A S T I C
PROFESSIONAL BOOKS

NEW YORK • TORONTO • LONDON • AUCKLAND • SYDNEY

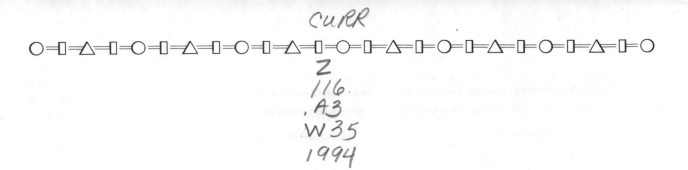

Over the last decade I have worked with hundreds of teachers and students,
showing them how to make books. I dedicate this book to them and
to Edith Winthrop, director of the Westchester Teacher Center Institute.

A special thanks
to my husband, George,
my son, Chris,
and my dear friend Vilma Smith,
all three of whom have
helped me in countless ways.

Scholastic Inc. grants teachers permission to photocopy the reproducible patterns from this book for classroom use. No other part of this publication may be reproduced in whole or in part, or stored in a retrieval system, or transmitted in any form or by any means, electronic or mechanical, photocopying, recording, or otherwise, without written permission of the publisher. For information regarding permission, write to Scholastic Inc., 555 Broadway, New York, NY 10012-3999.

Designed by Jacqueline Swensen
Cover design by Vincent Ceci
Cover illustration by Susan Pizzo
Interior illustration by Carmen Robert Sorvillo

ISBN 0-590-49647-6

12 11 10 9 8 7 6 5 4 3   4 5/9

Copyright © 1994 by Scholastic Inc.

Printed in U.S.A.

22696

○−▯−△−▯−○−▯−△−▯−○−▯−△−▯−○−▯−△−▯−○−▯−△−▯−○−▯−△−▯−○

Table of Contents

Introduction

*M*aking Books across the Curriculum is packed with information on publishing student work in the classroom.

From the teacher's perspective, book-making enhances stories and reports, motivates students, reinforces units of study and is easy to achieve.

A salient feature of this book is that the examples were selected because they correspond to curriculum topics. This book provides ideas for creative covers, and pop-up pages, as well as books for little stories, holidays, and gifts. These are tried and true ideas that other teachers have successfully used in the classroom.

"It's incredibly exciting to have kids of all ages making books," said Sande Lyttle, an elementary school teacher. And it's an excitement the students feel too.

"They want to make book covers for their stories and they want to share these books with each other," said Harol Pesuit, a primary grade teacher. In her experience, even less fluent readers are eager to read their own words. Reading their books to an interested audience builds confidence and self-esteem.

Barbara Guglielmo, a second grade teacher, has found that book-making motivates writers as well. "Pop-ups are especially good for my reluctant writers. They are better able to focus their writing by working page-by-page along with each pop-up. It keeps them on track." Practice with writing skills is a natural component of book-making that doesn't have to be limited to creative stories. While there are dozens of designs inside these pages for creative work, there are equally as many suggestions for book-making with class reports and with subjects such as social studies, multicultural studies, math and science.

One second grade teacher had her class do a science report on dinosaurs. "They looked up dinosaurs, selected one in particular and then wrote a report. I showed them how to make the center-opening book, and they did beautiful art work for the cover. The enthusiasm for the report's written work was very high. And I believe it was because they enjoyed illustrating their work and making a book."

Many of the book designs in the following pages are easy to accomplish. Of course, young students will need help but by the third grade most of the necessary skills will be within their grasp. Some books, however, are more complicated, and school districts and teachers have come up with several creative solutions, such as:

○ The Publishing Center, manned by volunteers who make book covers, type the child's work and "publish" books.

○ Parent volunteers who, working at home, make just the book covers. Teachers have the children write and illustrate their work, and the work is then inserted into the premade book and stapled together by the teacher. "This year I have twenty-two students. The parents who volunteer make it possible for me to make books for everyone," said Mary Gallagher, an elementary school teacher.

One working mother said she liked volunteering for book-making because she could fit it into her busy schedule. "The teacher puts the supplies, instructions and a sample book into an envelope that comes home with my daughter. I cut, fold, paste and make the books in the evening. My daughter is thrilled that I'm helping and I like being involved."

○ Community groups can be involved too. Church groups, seniors and older students can make the books. One den leader thought it was a perfect "community service project for the Girl Scouts."

As you go through the book, you will notice that with each design there are suggestions on literature and content area tie-ins. Of course, you will think of more and find ways to use the methods shown to make your own designs.

NOTE: Both templates and step-by-step instructions are provided for almost every book design. This is because sometimes you will need the ease of templates and other times you will want to read the instructions to your class and let them create the book design themselves. The choice is yours—feel free to use the method best for your students and you, and adapt as you wish.

Enjoy yourself and let those creative juices flow. I look forward to hearing from you and, of course, send pictures!

—Natalie Walsh

Supplies

Templates: The templates will work with paper smaller than 8 3/8 x 10 7/8, which is the size of this book. If you choose to use the step-by-step directions without templates, the measurements will produce a slightly larger book. There are no templates for the minibooks.

Most of the supplies needed are standard in the classroom:

○ scissors

○ crayons, felt-tip markers, watercolor paints or colored pencils

○ pencils

○ rulers

○ glue

○ construction paper

○ tag board *

○ long-reach stapler

○ recycled wallpaper books and brown paper bags

○ special items such as cloth tape, filament tape, mounting board, fabric and ribbon are needed on occasion and will be listed under materials for that book design.

* Tag board is an essential. Tag board is 150-pound-weight white paper available through many school suppliers. It is very similar to manila folders in texture and weight. It is *not* oak tag or poster board, both of which are generally unsuitable because of their stiffness and inability to crease well.

A terrific tool to have is a long-reach stapler. With it you will be able to staple up to 12 inches in from the edge of the paper. It is essential equipment for easy classroom publishing.

For some of the books, recycled items are required and are usually available free. Discarded wallpaper books are generally available from paint and hardware stores. For the base cover of the cloth books, used cardboard boxes are cut down to size.

Basic Book-Binding Techniques

These are the techniques that will enable you to make dozens of different kinds of books. You can use these techniques on their own without the other ideas in this book. But, more important, knowing these techniques will give you the creative edge as you begin to make the books in the chapters that follow.

For example, there will be times when one student just writes and writes about a particular subject, creating a hefty manuscript. You find you can't bind the book with the method you had planned. *But* because you know there's more than one way to bind a book, you create an extended cover for this prolific writer.

I call this Plan B. Knowing how and when to move into Plan B will give you confidence.

Another advantage of four of the techniques that follow—the strip-hinge, extending cover, cloth book and wallpaper cover book—is that they can be made in advance by volunteers and stored for when the teacher needs them. This makes book-making with thirty students relatively easy to accomplish. And how proud the students are to have their work "published!"

Strip-hinge Cover

The three biggest advantages of this method: the young writer can illustrate the cover, parent volunteers can make many of these book covers ahead of time and have them available for the teachers, and "It's simple but lends formality to the work," in the words of Harol Pesuit, second grade teacher.

MATERIALS: tag board, filament tape, scissors, ruler, stapler.

1 - Cut two pieces of tag board in half into 9-by-6-inch rectangles.

2 - Take one of those rectangles and measure 1/2 inch off the 6-inch length. Cut this strip off.

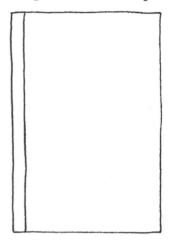

3 - Tape this strip back onto where you cut it off using filament tape and leaving an 1/8-inch gap between the strip and the tag board.

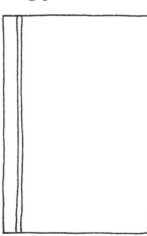

4 - Put the taped side to the inside of book.

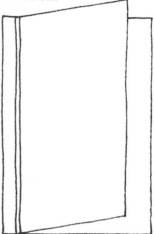

5 - Insert student's work and staple in the bendable margins. Brads can be placed through the strip if the written work is too long for a stapler to go through.

Extending Cover

The biggest advantage of the extending cover is that it expands to meet the needs of the prolific young writer or illustrator. Other advantages:

○ A student can illustrate the cover by using drawing paper instead of wallpaper and then covering the book with clear Con-Tact paper.

○ It is a good scrap book, photo album or journal.

○ It can be made ahead of time with a wallpaper cover and stored until needed.

MATERIALS: cardboard, glue, scissors, cloth tape, wallpaper, hole punch, 30-inch ribbon, or shoelace. The paper used for the inside pages will vary depending on how the book will be used. For a scrap book or photo album, white construction paper is appropriate. For a story, use 8 1/2-by-11-inch sheets of white paper folded in half.

1 - Cut two pieces of cardboard into 9-by-6 1/4-inch rectangles. From each piece, cut a strip 1 inch by 9 inches.

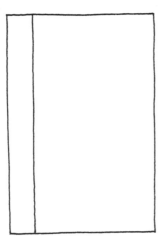

2 - Tape each strip back to the 9-by-5 1/4-piece leaving a 1/8-inch space between pieces.

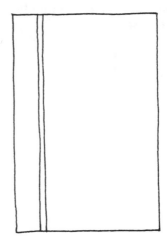

3 - To make this cover, each side of the book is treated independently. Cut two pieces of matching wallpaper 10 1/2 inches by 7 3/4 inches. There should be 3/4 inch extending past the edges all around. Cut two more pieces of a coordinating paper 8 5/8 by 5 7/8 inches.

4 - Place one of the large sheets of wallpaper face down on the table and glue the cardboard as shown in the illustration.

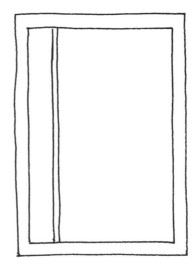

5 - Miter corners and glue down all edges.

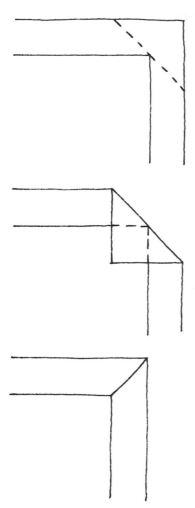

6 - Center inside piece of wallpaper on cover and glue down.

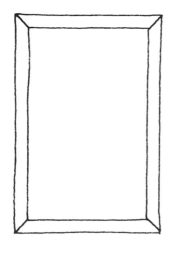

7 - Repeat steps 4, 5 and 6 for other side of cover.

8 - After it is dried, use a hole punch and make three holes on the strip through both covers and the written work.

9 - Lace through the holes and tie.

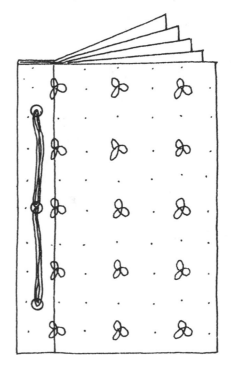

Back-to-Back Construction

A simple way to make pop-up books. With this method each page of the pop-up book is made separately. Once all the pop-up pages and written work are completed, they are organized page-after-page and bound together by gluing the back of one page to the back of the next page.

MATERIALS: Completed pop-up pages, glue, construction paper and scissors.

1 - Each illustration and written page of a pop-up book is folded in half.

2 - The pages are then glued back-to-back to each other forming a book. For example, the back of the right side of page 2 would be glued to the back of the left side of page 3. It is best to glue around the edges. Caution: don't let glue near a movable part of the pop-up or it will be a pop-down!

3 - Cover with a large sheet of construction paper trimmed to size. How big a piece will depend upon how many pages are in the finished book.

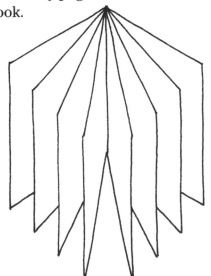

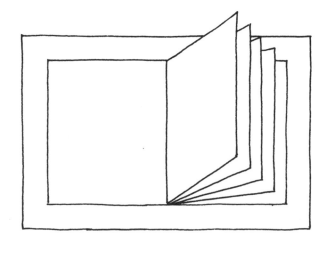

4 - Complete by writing the title and author on the front cover.

Wallpaper-Cover Book

The advantages of this book are the following: it is easy to make, it can be made ahead of time by volunteers, it is pretty, colorful and easy to clean.

MATERIALS: tag board (9-by-12-inch sheet), glue, one sheet of wallpaper 10 1/2 by 14 1/2 inches for cover, one piece of wallpaper 8 1/2 by 12 1/2 inches for inside of cover, glue, scissors, stapler and 8 1/2-by-11-inch white paper.

1 - Cut tag board into 2 pieces 5 1/4 by 9 and 2 strips 3/4 inch by 9.

2 - Place large piece of wallpaper good side down on table. Mark 3/4 inch border on all four sides.

3 - Lay tag board on wallpaper as in illustration, leaving 1/2 inch space in center and 1/4 inch between strips. Put a pencil mark on the wallpaper at each corner of the tag board pieces. This will help you line up each piece as you glue the pieces to the wallpaper. Glue pieces down.

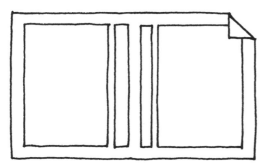

4 - Miter corners of wallpaper and secure with glue.

5 - Glue edges down.

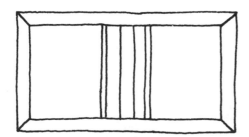

6 - Place smaller piece of wallpaper evenly over inside of book and secure with glue.

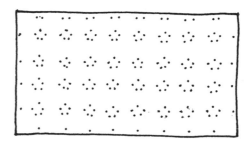

7 - Fold book in half. Insert story pages and staple at bendable margins.

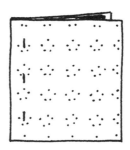

Cloth Book

A lovely book that is a pleasure to hold. The cover is inviting and soft to the touch. The ribbon tie gives a sense of privacy making this a great choice for a personal journal. It is especially appealing and makes a fine present for a holiday, particularly if you choose fabrics with novelty prints, such as black cats for a Halloween book, wreaths for Christmas, or little hearts for Valentine's Day.

It is also possible for older students to make these books for younger grades or as a fundraiser for a class project.

MATERIALS: two pieces of cardboard 5 inches by 9 inches, two cardboard strips 3/4 inch by 9 inches, 9-by-12 1/2-inch piece of polyester batting, glue, ribbon (optional), wallpaper (12 1/4 by 8 1/2 inches), scissors, 11-by-14 1/2-inch piece of fabric, needle, heavy duty thread and 8 1/2-by-11-inch white paper.

1 - Place fabric good side down on table and center polyester batting on it. Place cardboard evenly over batting as in illustration leaving 1/2 inch gap in center and 1/4 inch gap between strips.

2 - Glue cardboard to polyester batting. DO NOT GLUE BATTING TO FABRIC.

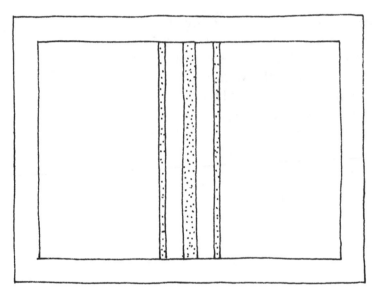

3 - Fold fabric over the edges; miter corners first, then glue all around.

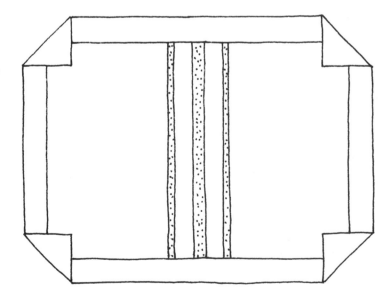

4 - Optional. Take a 36-inch piece of ribbon and place across the middle of the book making sure the lengths of the strands extending beyond the cover are even. Glue the ribbon that straddles the cardboard to the cardboard.

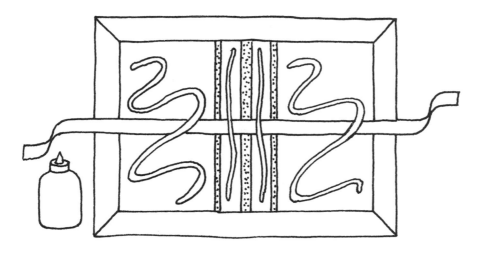

5 - Cut piece of wallpaper 12 1/4 by 8 1/2 inches for the inside of cover. Center wallpaper on inside cover and glue. About 1/4 inch of the cover fabric will show around all the edges.

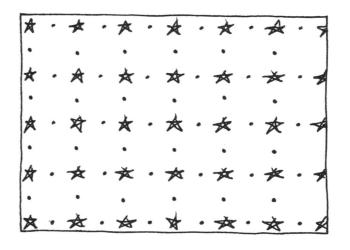

6 - To insert the pages of the book, fold three or four sheets of 8 1/2-by-11-inch white paper in half. Crease well. Center the paper in the book and sew with a running stitch, down the center through the paper and the spine of the book. Knot at end.

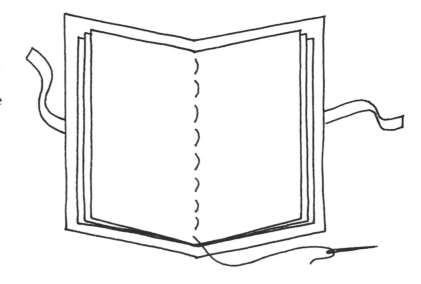

SEWING TIP: If you make your stitches inside the book large and the stitches that show through the cloth along the spine tiny, you will have a neater-looking book. Book can also be sewn on most sewing machines.

Shape Books

SHAPE BOOKS

There are three distinct types of shape books: straight shapes, stand-up shapes and shapes-on-the-fold.

Straight shapes can be bound by a strip-hinge, stapler, paper fasteners or ribbons. Which choice is best will be evident as we proceed. Stand-up shapes are great for displays because, as the name suggests, they stand on their own. And shapes-on-the fold are economical little books that use a minimum amount of supplies and are easy to make on a limited work area like a desktop.

The following shapes are suggestions chosen because of their versatility. However, the fun of shape books is in the creation. If you can think it, you can most likely make it into a shape book cover. Have fun. Be expressive.

I have included templates for the shape books and have also given step-by-step directions. I chose to provide this option because sometimes you will want the ease of a template, and other times you will want to read the directions step-by-step to your class, letting them create their version of the shape. The overwhelming advantage to the latter approach is that the finished books all look different . . . and there's something joyful in creativity expressed.

Think of shape books in terms of report writing too. On the pages that follow you'll see book shapes that lend themselves to all sorts of reports — from book reports to research reports.

For example, a student doing a history report on life on the American frontier in the 1800's could choose to make the Conestoga Wagon or use the house shape to make a log cabin typical of the period.

STRAIGHT SHAPES

The Bus

Templates on pages 20–21

The templates are meant to provide an outline that permits flexibility in designing the bus. Two templates for the bus are provided. The first has the windows and doors marked. The second template has no marked windows or doors, which gives great flexibility in designing the shape into a bus, car, or delivery truck.

MATERIALS: two pieces of tag board, scissors, ruler, utility knife (optional), stapler, crayons or felt-tip markers

1 - Begin to draw a bus by rounding off the top left corner on the tag board. Cut off.

2 - On the right edge of the paper put a dot along the edge 5 inches from the bottom of the page. Measure in 3 inches from this point into the page and draw a line.

3 - Draw a vertical line from the end of the 3 inches to the top of the paper. This will be the hood and windshield.

4 - Cut along those lines, rounding the corners.

5 - At the bottom of the page measure up 1 3/4 inches and draw a line. This is the bottom of the bus.

6 - For the windows and bus door, mark the point 5 inches up from the bottom of the paper.

7 - Lay the ruler across this point and measure. Each window is 1 1/2 inches wide with a 1/2 inch space between each starting from the left side of the page. The door is 1 1/4 inches wide.

8 - Each window is 2 inches tall. The door should extend to the bottom of the bus.

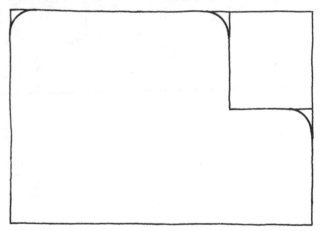

9 - Draw the wheels as in illustration. Cut out the area around the wheels.

10 - Decorate to complete. Use the first piece of tag board as a template and trace it onto a second piece of tag board. Cut out bus shape. This will be the back cover.

11 - For the inside pages use a folded 8 1/2-by-14-sheet of paper (legal size). Fold the paper in half from top to bottom. Crease well. Insert in between covers lining the work up at the top.

12 - The pages can be connected by simply stapling along the roof line of the bus. However, if the written work is too thick, a strip-hinge along the roof line will accommodate more pages. Strip-hinge directions are on page 7.

Ideas and Options

○ The bus door can easily open and close by making a flap. See page 75.

○ The windows can be cut out with an utility knife, and individual class photographs can be placed in the opening: family photos, too. Be sure to measure the photograph and adjust the window size if necessary. Use template without marked windows and door.

○ With a little pencil remodeling, this bus can also be the family station wagon or a delivery truck.

Literature

School Bus by Donald Crews

This is the Way We Go to School by Edith Baer

The Magic School Bus series by Joanna Cole

Wheels on the Bus by Raffi

Content Area Tie-ins

Transportation— school bus, city bus.

Family— the family car, members of a family, visiting relatives.

   The Relatives Came by Cynthia Rylant

   Just Us Women by Jeannette Caines

Community— delivery trucks, goods and services in the community.

Safety— safe street crossing, bus stop safety, proper conduct, traffic rules.

The bus can also become one of these:

Family Station Wagon

Delivery Truck

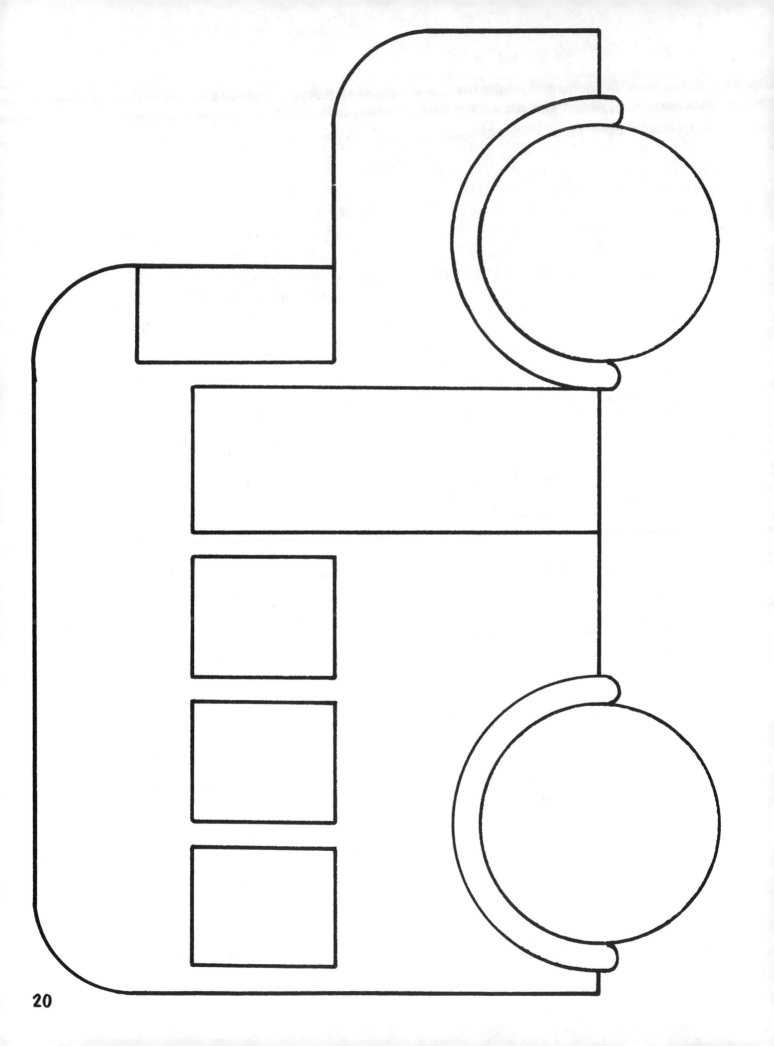

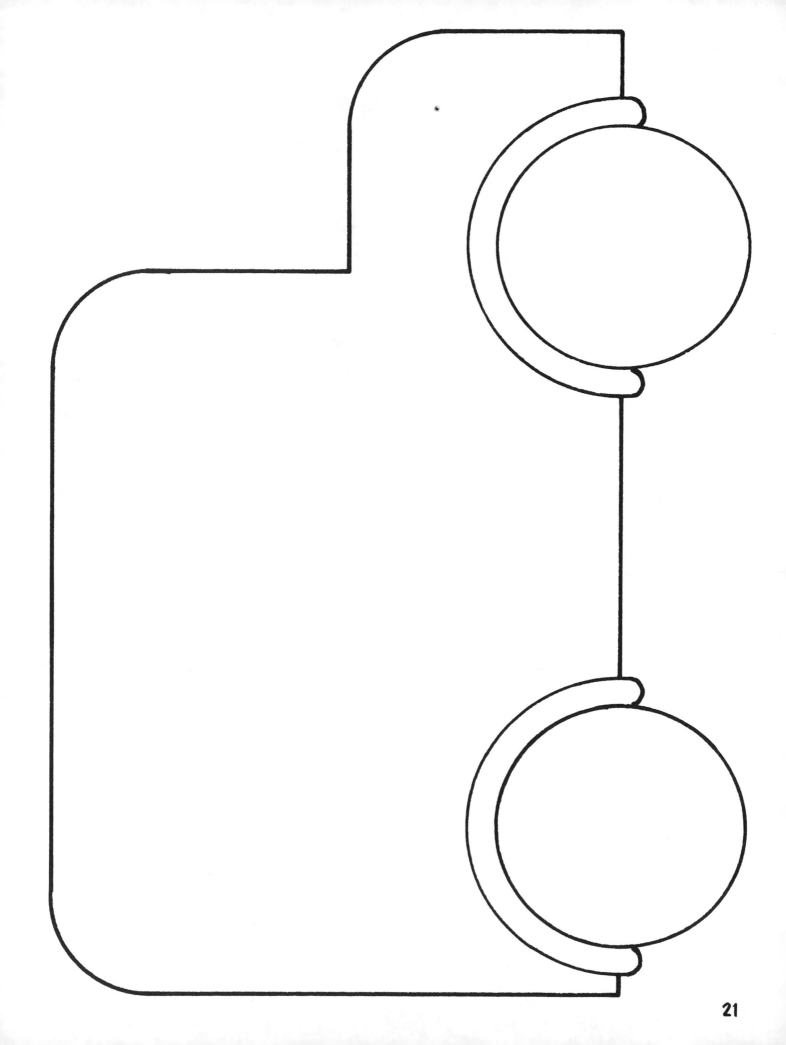

21

The Elephant

Templates on page 24–25

MATERIALS: two pieces of tag board, ribbon or stapler, crayons or felt-tip markers

1 - The body of the elephant without legs will go on the front piece of tag board. The body and legs go on the second piece.

2 - In the top seven inches of the page, draw the elephant. Drawing help: begin by drawing a large rounded oval head. Add ears, a trunk and a rounded body. Refine drawing. Cut the elephant out.

3 - Trace outline of first drawing on second piece of tag board, adding two hefty legs. Cut out the drawing, legs and all.

4 - Color the elephant.

5 - A book can be made by punching two small holes through the top of the head of both covers and the student's work, lacing a ribbon through the holes and tying a bow. This creates a lighthearted elephant suitable for younger grades.

For older students, the elephant book can be stapled at the ear or at the top of the head.

6 - An 8 1/2-by-11-inch sheet of paper folded in half from top to bottom will need minimum trimming to fit.

Ideas and Options

○ Although the example is an elephant, any two- or four-legged rounded creature will work, from puppies and kittens to lambs and lions to geese and pigs to bears and other beasts.

Literature

The Blind Men and the Elephant by Karen Backstein

Frank and Ernest by Alexandra Day

Babar the King by Jean de Brunhoff

Fables by Arnold Lobel

Sato and the Elephants by Juanita Havill

Elephants by Norman Barrett

The Elephant Book by Robert Leydenfrost

Content Area Tie-ins

Endangered species, Seasons (For March, make two books, one a lion and the other a lamb.)

Nursery rhymes (lamb, kitten, bear).

History—

Suleiman the Elephant by Margret Rettich

Old Bet and the Start of the American Circus by Robert M. McClung

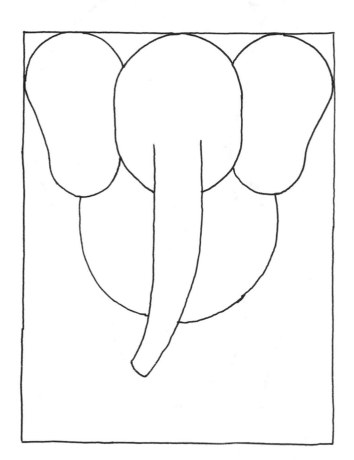

On first page of tag board, draw elephant without legs and cut out.

On second piece of tag board, trace front piece of tag board and add hefty legs

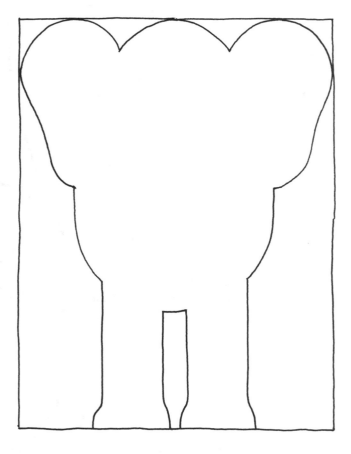

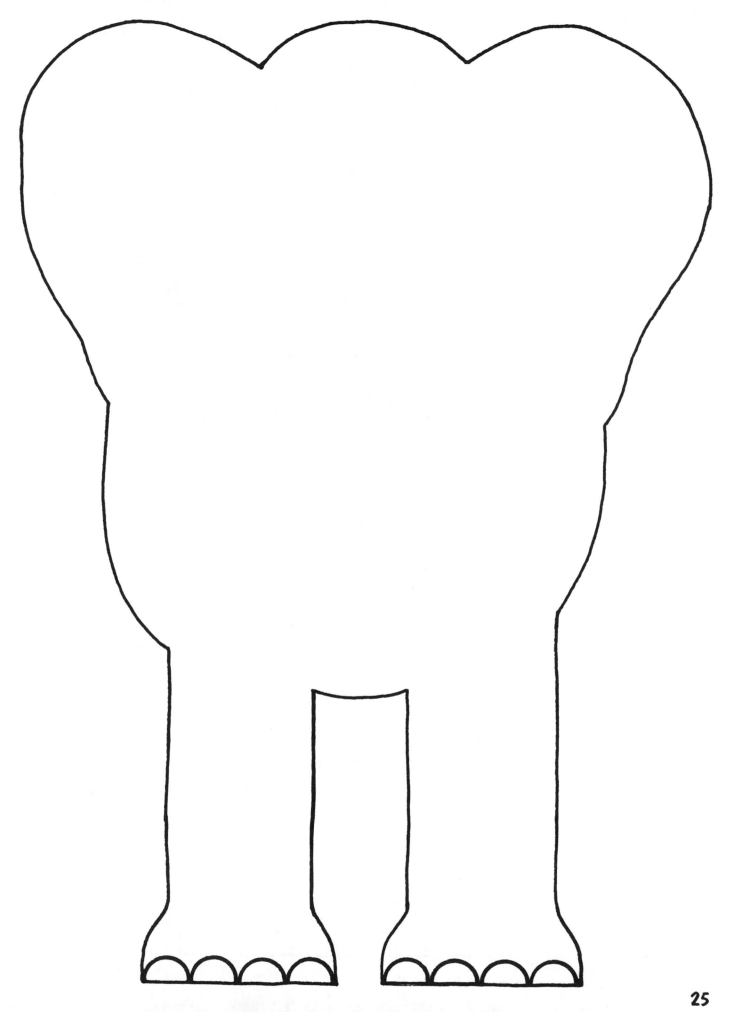

25

Conestoga Wagon

Template on page 28

MATERIALS: Two pieces of tag board, pencil, a compass, ruler, scissors, an 18-inch piece of string or leather shoelace, crayons, felt-tip markers or watercolor paints*

1 - Measure 2 inches up from the bottom of the page. Cut this strip off.

2 - Measure 2 1/2 inches from the new bottom up and draw a light line. This is the wooden section of the wagon.

3 - Along this line, mark 4 1/2 inches and 1/2 inch in from the right edge. These mark the top front corners of the wagon. Along the bottom of the page, measure in from the right edge 3 3/4 inches and 1 1/4 inches.

These mark the bottom front corners of the wagon. Connect the dots as in illustration.

For the back edges of the wagon, measure in from the edge 1 inch along the bottom and 1/2 inch along the line. Connect these dots.

4 - The front canvas section of the wagon billows up like an upside-down horseshoe. At its widest, the front canvas is about 5 inches from the right edge of the paper.

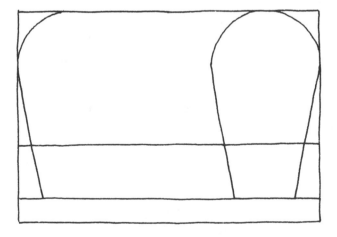

5 - Draw the remaining areas of the wagon following the illustration. Helpful note: The ribs of the wagon are about 1 inch apart.

6 - Color and cut out wagon.

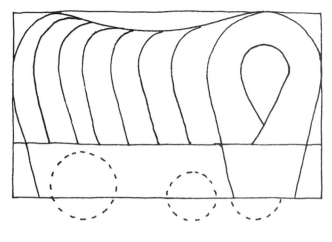

7 - From another piece of tag board, cut out the back wheel (3 1/2 inches in diameter) and the front wheel (3 inches in diameter). Cut a third wheel, also 3 inches in diameter, for the back of the front section of the wagon to add dimension.

8 - Color wheels and glue them to wagon.

9 - Trace wagon, wheels and all, onto the back piece of tag board and cut out.

10 - To bind the book, start by inserting inside pages (full-size 8 1/2-by-11-inch sheets of paper can be trimmed to fit). Put cover in place and, using a sharp point, punch through book six times at the ribs along the top of the canvas. Next, lace all pages through with string or leather shoelaces and tie off.

Literature

The Little House on the Prairie by Laura Ingalls Wilder

Kate's Book by Mary Francis Shura

Wagon Wheel by Barbara Brenner

My Prairie Year: Based on the diary of Elenore Plaisted by Brett Harvey

Cassie's Journey: Going West in the 1860's by Brett Harvey

Grandma Essie's Covered Wagon by David Williams

Go West by Martin Waddell

Content Area Tie-ins

Frontier life, The gold rush, America in the 1800's.

*Watercolor paints work very nicely on tag board.

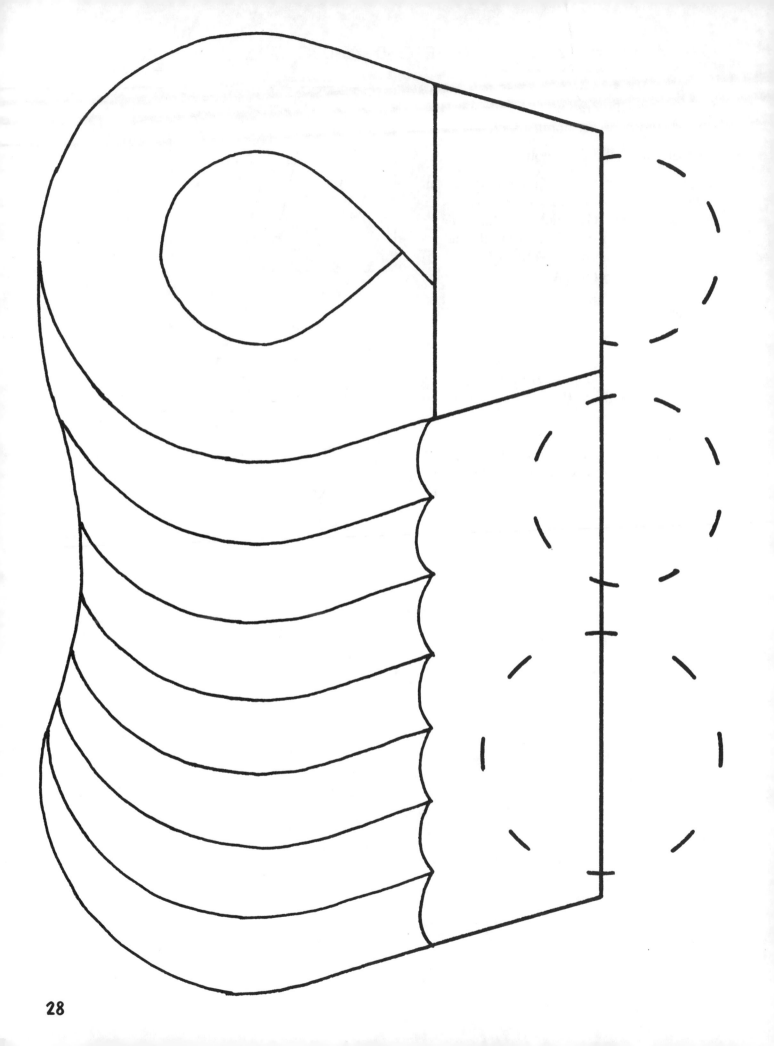

Doll

Template on page 30

Using the template, lightly trace the doll outline onto tag board. This same outline can be an astronaut, a rag doll, a gingerbread man, or a pioneer girl. The template outline is meant to *suggest* the form. Your students add the details. The trick to making a nice-size book is to make the clothing bulky. Encourage them to add accessories and a hair style before cutting the figure out.

MATERIALS: crayons, felt-tip markers, tag board, scissors, stapler, ribbon (optional)

1 - Using the template as a basic form, draw your subject. Add clothing or accessories pertinent to the figure. For example, a back-pack might be drawn on the astronaut.

2 - Draw figure and color.

3 - Cut the figure out.

4 - The cutout figure is used as a template for cutting out the interior pages of the book as well as the back cover and ideally uses most of an 8 1/2-by-11-inch piece of paper.

5 - Attach all pages by stapling through hand, using a brad or tying a ribbon through a hole punched through the hand.

Literature

When the Dolls Woke by Marjorie F. Stover
The Story of Holly and Ivy by Rumer Godden

The Legend of Bluebonnet by Tomie dePaola
William's Doll by Charlotte Zolotow
Three Young Pilgrims by Cheryl Harness

Content Area Tie-ins

Community— make individual family members, career people or children from around the globe.

Nursery rhyme, fairy tale characters— such as the Gingerbread Man, Little Bo-Peep, Little Red Riding Hood, Goldilocks.
The Gingerbread Boy by Paul Galdone
The Helen Oxenbury Nursery Story Book (*Goldilocks and the Three Bears*, *The Gingerbread Man*, *Little Red Riding Hood*)

Space exploration— Astronaut.
The Picture World of Astronauts by Norman Barrett
Sally Ride: America's First Woman in Space by Carolyn Blacknall
The Three Astronauts by Umberto Eco and Eugenio Carmi

American History— Colonial people.
The Pilgrim's First Thanksgiving by Ann McGovern
If You Lived In Colonial Times by Ann McGovern

Multicultural— Various characters.
Babushka's Doll by Patricia Polacco
Molly's Pilgrim by Barbara Cohen

House

Template on page 33

This template provides the basic form of a house. It can be any house, including a log cabin, or an old schoolhouse. With the latter, a bell tower was drawn in before the house was cut out. It could just as easily become a church by drawing on a steeple, or a barn by drawing on big red doors and open windows.

Ideas and Options

○ Have the students show how a house might change over time, with some of the students drawing how people made houses in the 1700s and another group drawing how houses are made today.

○ Instead of a finished house, the skeletal frame of the house could be drawn showing how homes are constructed.

MATERIALS: tag board, scissors, brads, hole punch, crayons, felt-tip markers, watercolor paints or colored pencils

1 - Trace template on two pieces of tag board for front and back covers.

2 - Decide what kind of house you are creating and add details, for example, a belfry for a one-room schoolhouse.

3 - Finish drawing and coloring the house.

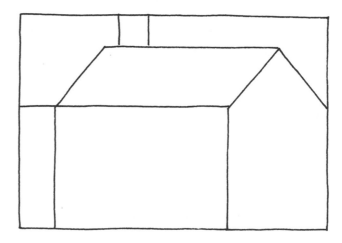

4 - Cut out both pieces, Note that the extra space between the end of the house and the left side of the page is where the book will be bound. Do not cut this strip off.

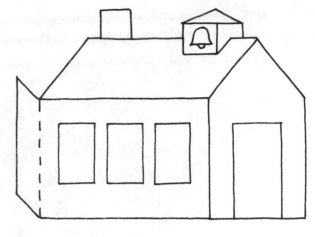

5 - On both covers, fold strip at end of house to crease.

6 - Putting the right sides together, punch 3 holes through both flaps.

7 - Bend flaps to the inside of the book, mark and punch holes through pages using the cover holes as a guide.

8 - Attach with brads. The brads do not show through the cover but are on the inside of the front page.

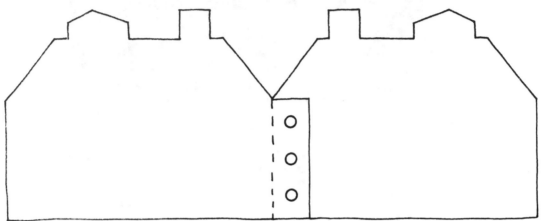

Literature

The New House by Joyce Maynard

Building a House by Byron Barton

The Little House by Virginia Lee Burton

A House is a House for Me by Mary Ann Hoberman

Need a House? Call Mrs. Mouse by George Mendoza

Meanwhile Back at the Ranch by Trinka Hakes Noble

Content Area Tie-ins

Community—

Where the Children Live by Thomas B. Allen

World History—

Visiting a Village by Bobbie Kalman

American History— colonial house, log cabin, schoolhouse

If you Lived in Colonial Times by Ann McGovern

Lincoln: A Photobiography by Russell Freedman

Little House on the Prairie by Laura Ingalls Wilder

Log Cabin in the Woods - A True Story About a Pioneer Boy by Joanne L. Henry

Multicultural Studies—

Keepers of the Earth by Michael J. Caduto and Joseph Bruchac

The Village of Round and Square Houses by Ann Grifalconi

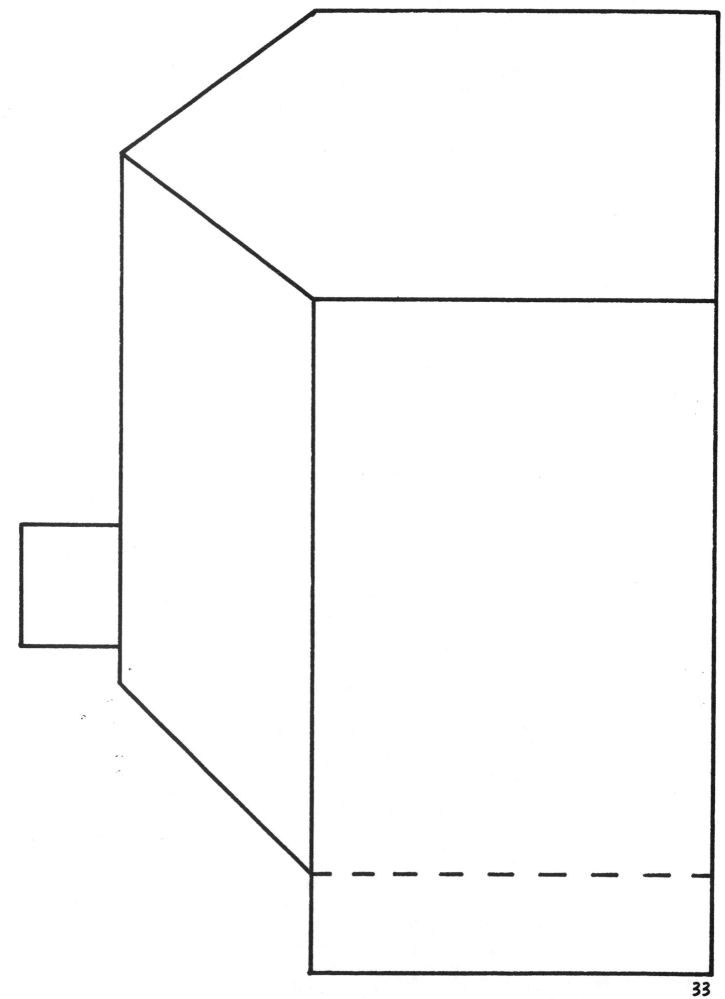

STAND-UP SHAPES

This is a fun design that can be a person, an animal or a tree!

The advantages of this book form are the following:

○ These books are great for displays, as they actually stand up.

○ They can also be used on a bulletin board.

○ They can be made to recall a particular time, such as when the child had chicken pox or a particular person, for example, when doing a report on George Washington.

○ And, with a little ingenuity, they can be a gift when you turn the index cards into redeemable coupons.

○ All written work is done on index cards and attached to the stand-up shape as one of the last steps.

Stand-up Person

Template on page 36

The template provides a general outline of the head, shoulder and arms. Students should draw their own figure using the template as a guide and adding hair and other features before cutting the figure out.

MATERIALS: tag board, ruler, 3-by-5-inch index cards, stapler, crayons or felt-tip markers, yarn for hair, string, "googly eyes," etc.

1 - Trace template for general outline of head, shoulders and arms.

2 - Using template outline as a guide, create your figure. Be sure to add hair, hat or other accessories.

3 - Color figure completely and cut out. Color both the front and back of the arms. Option: cut hands out of tag board scraps and glue in place.

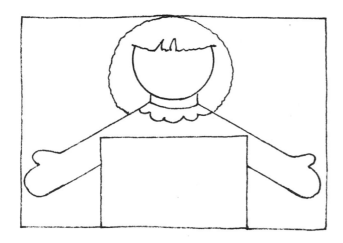

Use template as outline; add hair style. Color. Then cut away background.

4 - Center 3-by-5-inch index cards along bottom and staple along top edge to tag board. Use at least three cards but no more than six.

5 - Fold tag board behind the index cards back to create a stand. Figure will stand up.

6 - Fold arms in front of cards.

7 - From the cutout scraps, objects can be cut out and added to the hands—for example, a pencil for a writer, a doll for a child, a hat for a gentleman, a sports ball for an athlete.

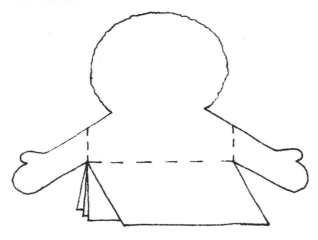

Literature and Content Area Tie-ins

Multicultural studies—
The Lily Cupboard by Shulamith Oppenheim
Apple Pie and Onions by Judith Caseley

People with Disabilities—
Someone Special, Just Like You by Tricia Brown
Stay Away from Simon by Carol Carrick

Ideas and Options

○ Nice displays of different occupations can be created.

○ Books that focus on ethnic groups, different communities, historical figures, and heroes are other possibilities.

○ These books can also be used as gifts by featuring child's caregiver or grandparents with the index cards telling why they are appreciated.

○ The grandparents can relate a story about the family's history, what the world was like when they were nine years old, or what it was like when Grandpa was courting Grandma. These personal histories could be fun and would provide practice with many skills from listening to planning to writing.

○ This book can also be a book about why the child is special, including his/her likes and dislikes, best day, worst day, or as a remembrance of the time he or she had chicken pox. Read *Itchy, Itchy Chicken Pox* by Grace Maccarone.

○ It could also be used to depict a nursery rhyme or fairy tale character. Or, with mythology, it could be made to resemble a particular character.

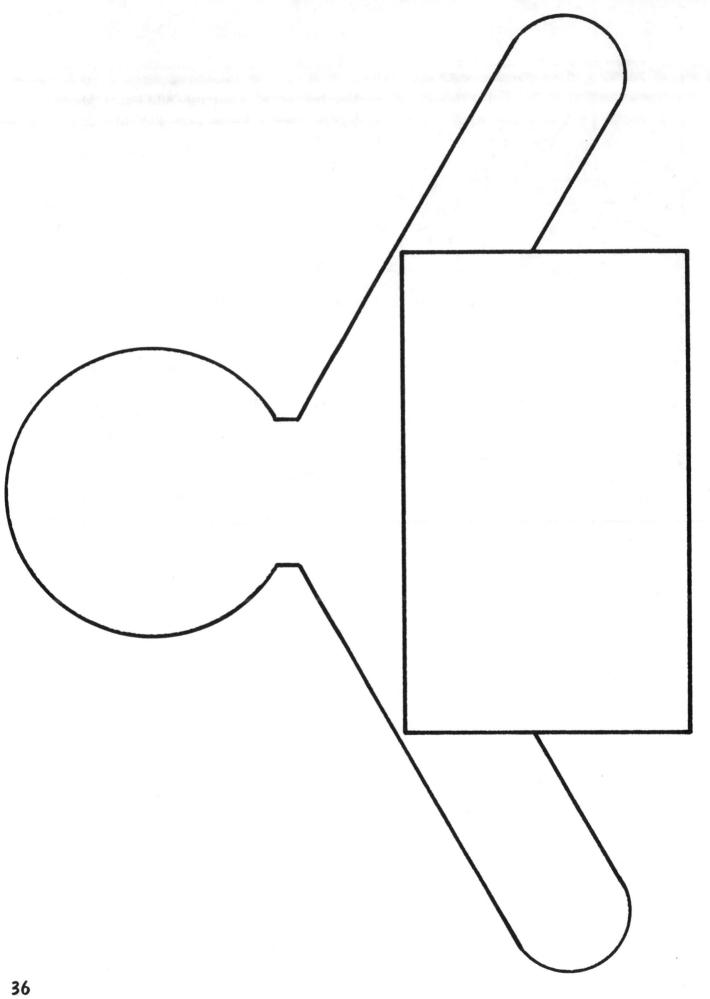

Stand-up Evergreen Tree

Template on page 41

This design can be made as a special holiday gift with the index card "coupons" redeemable for tasks the child is willing to do: for example, read a book to baby brother, clear the table, sort the socks, check in on an elderly neighbor.

MATERIALS: one piece of tag board, five 3-by-5-inch index cards, construction paper, scissors, stapler, crayons, felt-tip markers or watercolor paints. Glitter is optional.

1 - Trace template onto tag board.

2 - Color, and cut out. You can be fancy and use glitter to make Christmas balls, or brightly colored balls can be made with a hole punch and construction paper.

3 - Cut out tree.

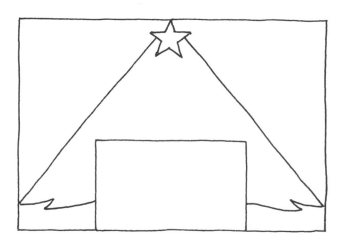

4 - On one unlined index card, draw a gift box. (You can use the back of a lined index card). The student can draw "To" and "From" tags. On the other 3-by-5-inch index cards, the students write what they are willing to do as their gift.

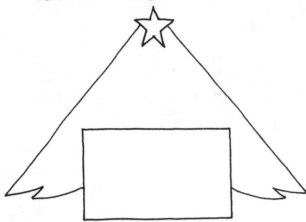

5 - The index cards are centered at the bottom of the page, and stapled along the top of the cards to the tree.

6 - Fold area of tree behind the index cards back to form support. Tree will stand.

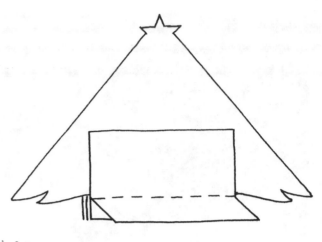

Literature

Christmas Trees by Robert Frost

The After-Christmas Tree by Linda Wagner Tyler

Hans Andersen's Fairy Tales translated by L.W. Kingsland

Christmas Tree Memories by Aliki

Why Christmas Trees Aren't Perfect by Richard H. Schneider

Night Tree by Eve Bunting

Content Area Tie-ins

Plant life, environmental studies.

Once There was a Tree by Natalia Romanova

Whisper from the Woods by Victoria Wirth

Trees by Ruth Thomson

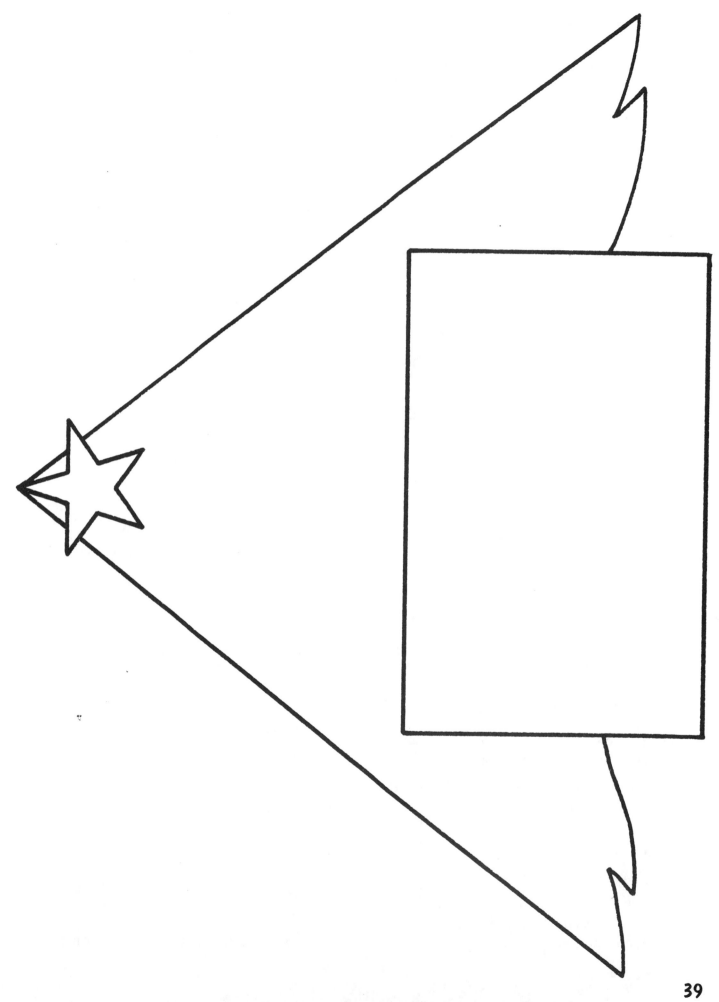

Stand-Up Bear

Template on page 41

MATERIALS: one piece of tag board, 3-by-5-inch index cards, construction paper, scissors, stapler, crayons, felt-tip markers or watercolor paints.

1 - Trace template onto tag board.

2 - Color and cut out. Be sure to color both sides of bear's arms.

3 - Center index cards at the bottom of the tag board (see template), and staple along the top of the cards to the bear.

4 - Fold bear's arms around index cards.

5 - Fold back the area of bear behind the index cards to form support. Bear will stand.

6 - Optional: add something to bear's hands. (A honey jar?)

Literature

Bear by John Schoenherr

Bear Shadow by Frank Asch

Goldilocks and the Three Bears retold by James Marshall

Jamberry by Bruce Degen

Fat Man in a Fur Coat and Other Bear Stories by Alvin Schwartz

Ira Sleeps Over by Bernard Waber

Brown Bear, Brown Bear. What Do You See? by Bill Martin Jr.

The Biggest Bear by Lynd Ward

A Bear Called Paddington by Michael Bond.

Content Area Tie-ins

American History, Multicultural studies—

The Bears of Alaska in Life and Legend by Jess Rennicke

Giving Voice to Bear: North American Myths, Rituals and Images of the Bear by David Rockwell

Corduroy by Don Freeman

Science, endangered species—

A Closer Look at Bears and Pandas by Bibby Whittaker

Bears by Michael Leach

Holidays—

The Chanukkah Guest by Eric Kimmel

SHAPES-ON-THE-FOLD

Although these books take two different forms they share a common factor: they are made with a single piece of tag board folded in half. In form number one the design is cut through both sides of the folded tag board, as in the apple book on page 44. In form two, the design is cut out only on the front cover, as in the apple book on page 45. In the latter case, the back cover remains a solid 9-by-6-inch rectangle connected at the fold to the front cover.

One of the pleasures of this book cover is that it is easy to make at a desk since it involves only one piece of paper and no glue. It is also simple to bind with a long-reach stapler.

Apple

Templates on pages 44–45

Although the sample is an apple, it could just as easily be other rounded fruits or vegetables, from oranges to turnips.

MATERIALS: tag board, crayons, scissors, long-reach stapler

1 - Fold tag board in half.

2 - Draw an apple, making sure the bottom remains straight so it can stand.

3 - Cut out the apple through both thicknesses.

4 - Color both the front and back cover with crayons, felt pens or watercolor paints.

5 - For the inside of the front cover, draw the core and seeds as if the apple is sliced open.

6 - 3-by-5-inch index cards can be used as pages by stapling them to the back cover or pages can be cut into the apple shape and stapled along the crease.

Ideas and Options

This idea offers lots of possibilities. The example could just as easily be a peach, a potato, a pumpkin, a cookie or even a slice of bread. The trick is butting the drawing up against the fold, providing a firm spine for the book.

Literature:

Apples—

An Apple a Day by Judi Barrett

The Apple Tree by Lynley Dodd

Apple Trees by Sylvia Johnson

Apple Tree by Barrie Watts

Frannie's Fruits by Leslie Kimmelman

Fairy Tales and Folk Tales—

Grimm's Fairy Tales (Snow White) by Jacob Grimm.

The Story of Johnny Appleseed by Aliki

Johnny Appleseed: A Tall Tale by Steven Kellogg

Seasons—

The Seasons of Arnold's Apple Tree by Gail Gibbons

Holiday—

Apple Tree Christmas by Trinka Hakes Noble

Multicultural—

Apple Pie and Onions by Judith Caseley

Community—

The Giving Tree by Shel Silverstein.

Peach—

James and the Giant Peach by Roald Dahl

Pumpkin—

The Biggest Pumpkin Ever by Steven Kroll

Oh, What a Thanksgiving by Steven Kroll

Pumpkin Pumpkin by Jeanne Titherington

Slice of Bread—

Bread Bread Bread by Ann Morris

Bread and Jam for Frances by Russell Hoban

Tony's Bread by Tomie DePaola

The Giant Jam Sandwich by John V. Lord and Janet Burroway

Cookie—

If You Give a Mouse a Cookie by Laura Jaffe Numeroff

Potato—

James O'Rourke and the Big Potato by Tomie DePaola

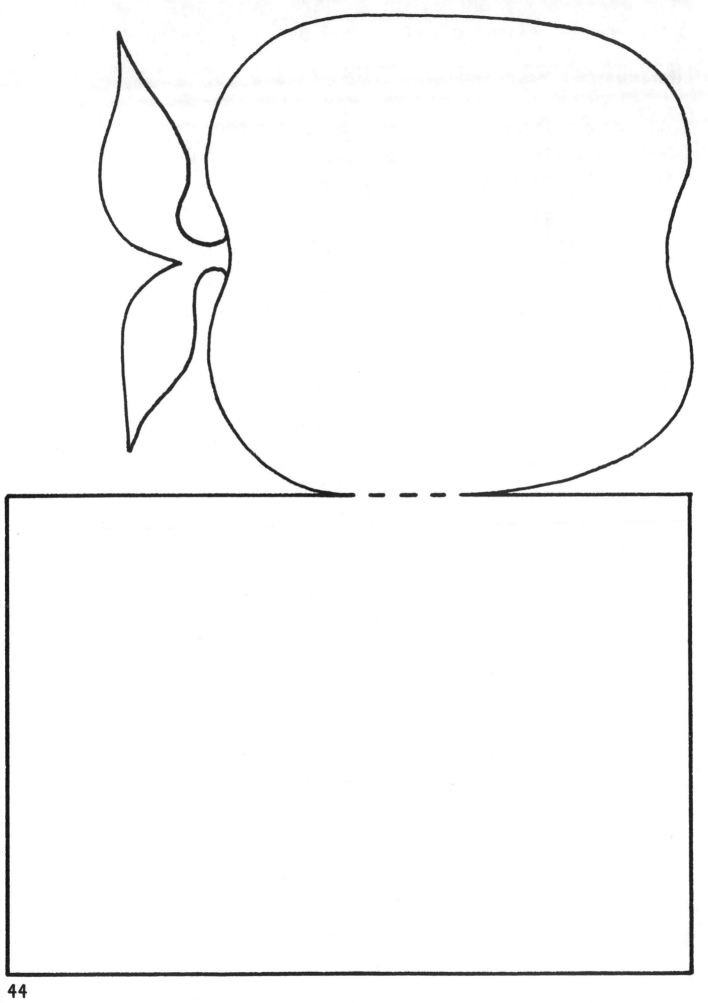

44

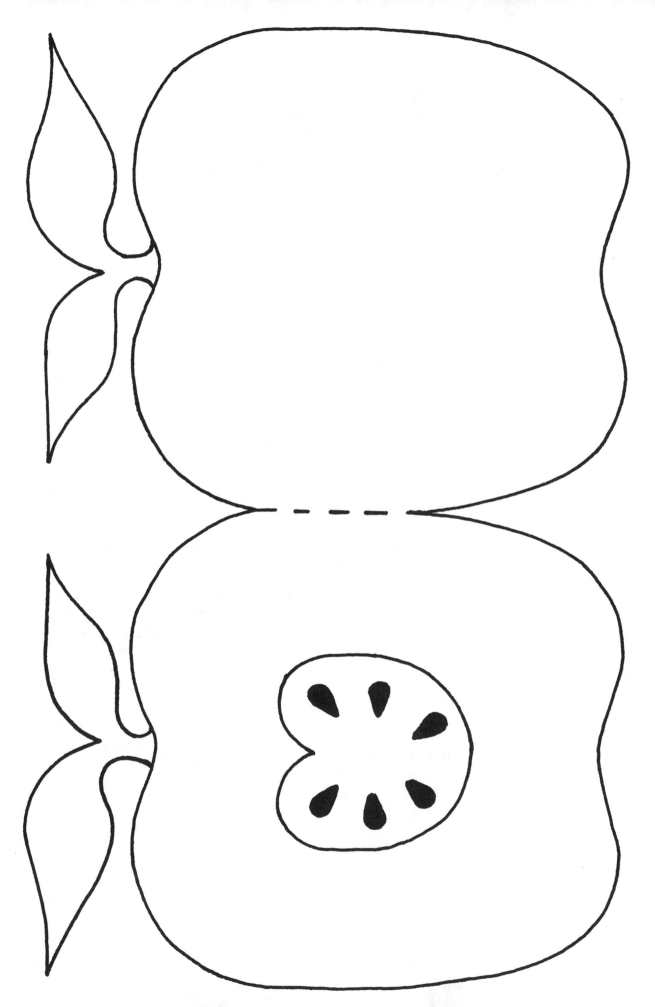

Quilt Square

Templates on pages 49–50

This book can be an easy afternoon project or part of a much larger unit involving the use of fractions, color and symmetry. The simplest approach would be to have each student design a square of fabric by coloring on a precut square. A more involved approach would be to have the students work with fractions and design a quilt square. A grid is provided on page 49 to help with this process.

There are hundreds of possible quilt patterns. You can have your students copy one from the page of suggestions that follows, or they can design their own. Either choice would provide great practice for their math skills. A third suggestion would be to use a quilt book with hundreds of patterns such as *500 Full-Size Patchwork Patterns* by Maggie Malone as a reference tool. Each student choosing and coloring his or her own "square" would make quite a quilt which can then be displayed on a bulletin board.

Deciding where to place the squares in the quilt—based on color and design—is also an interesting practice. Quilters know the arrangement of the squares is just as important as the squares themselves.

MATERIALS: tag board, scissors, crayons, felt-tip markers, ruler, pencil, long-reach stapler

1 - Fold tag board in half and cut 3 inches off the top, through both thicknesses, to create a 6-by-6-inch square cover.

2 - With the fold to the left, draw a single quilt square. There are many patterns, and each student could do the same pattern, or each can do a different pattern; the colors could be limited to a few hues or run the whole crayon box. There is a grid on page 49 to aid in making a symmetrical design.

3 - Fold 8 1/2-by-11-inch sheets of paper in half. Insert into cover and trim paper to fit. Staple to cover along crease.

4 - Display all finished quilt squares together on a bulletin board as a class quilt.

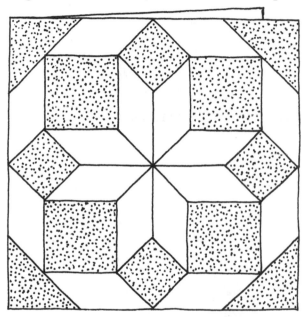

Literature

The Quilt Story by Tony Johnston

The Josefina Story Quilt by Eleanor Coerr

The Quilt by Ann Jonas

The Patchwork Quilt by Valerie Flournoy

The Keeping Quilt by Patricia Polacco

Content Area Tie-ins

History— women's skills in American history

Math— the study of symmetry, patterns, geometric shapes, fractions. There are numerous books of patterns available.

Art— Color harmony, complementary and opposite colors, spatial effect of colors.

Multicultural Studies— Each square could also represent a significant moment in the student's life or a moment from their family's history: e.g., when Great-Grandfather came from Europe. The written work could relate that family story. Read *Apple Pie and Onions* by Judith Caseley.

Another possibility is to look at quilts from around the world. See Robert Bishop's *Hands All Around: Quilts from Many Nations*.

Ideas and Options

○ Instead of a quilt, the square could be part of an African kente. Read *The Black Snowman* by Phil Mendez.

○ Another multicultural possibility would be for the square to be part of the rug being woven. Read *Annie and the Old One* by Miska Miles.

○ The students could copy the fabric from a favorite outfit of theirs for their square and write a story about something that happened when they wore that outfit.

○ Fractions— The different ways a square can be divided into four equal parts could make an interesting quilt.

Quilt Squares

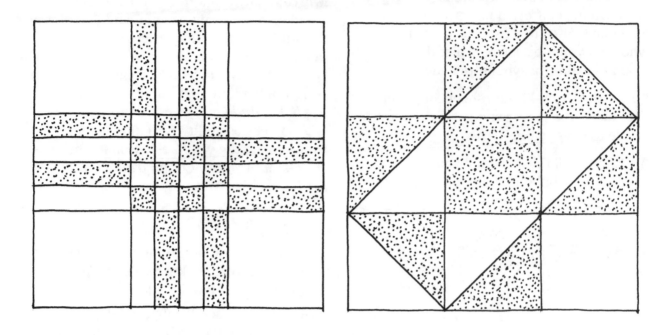

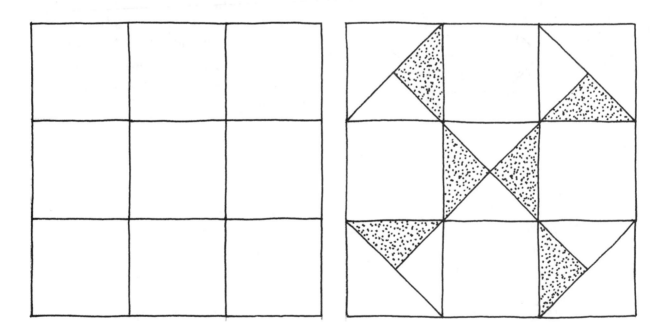

Nine Patch— This square changes dramatically with the use of light and dark squares.

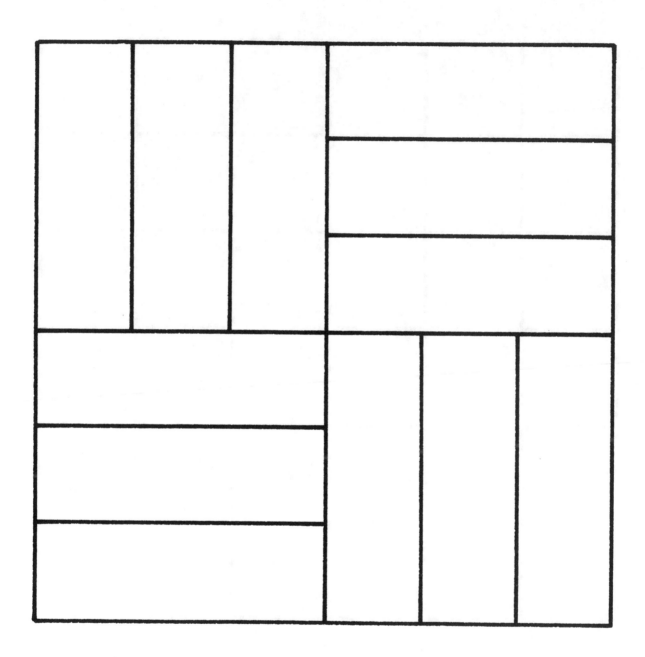

Dinosaur

Template on page 53

The template is for an Allosaurus. The protruding tail is an optional accessory that can be eliminated by simply drawing the tail along the back cover.

MATERIALS: tag board, scissors, crayons, markers, watercolor paints or colored pencils, long- reach stapler, construction paper

1 - Fold tag board in half. With fold facing to the left, draw your dinosaur or dragon. Have the drawing take up at least half of the cover.

2 - Color. Add construction paper leaves if desired.

3 - Cut around the figure but not between the figure and the fold. This is what adds stability to the cover. Do not cut back cover.

4 - Fold a piece of construction paper in half and insert into cover. Fold 8 1/2-by-11-inch sheets of paper in half and insert as pages. Staple on crease to complete.

To add optional tail

○ Cut out template tail and crease where marked.

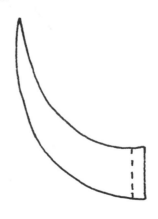

○ Cut slits along crease as in illustration.

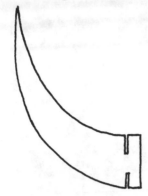

○ Make a 1-inch slit on fold of dinosaur book where the tail will go.

○ Fold tabs down to fit through the slit.

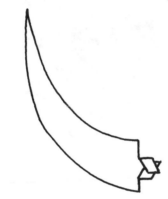

○ Open tabs on inside and tape in place.

Literature

Dinosaur Day by Liza Donnelly

Danny and the Dinosaur by Syd Hoff

Tyrannosaurus Was a Beast by Jack Prelutsky

Dinosaur Story by Joanna Cole

Digging Up Dinosaurs by Aliki

Cam Jansen and the Mystery of the Dinosaur Bones by David Adler

Ideas and Options:

This same basic design can be drawn to be a dragon.

Dragon Literature:

The Minstrel and the Dragon Pup by Rosemary Sutcliff

The Neverending Story by Michael Ende

Saint George and the Dragon by Margaret Hodges

Everyone Knows What a Dragon Looks Like by Jay Williams

I Hear A Noise by Diane Goode

My Father's Dragon by Ruth S. Gannett

The Dragon of an Ordinary Family by Margaret Mahy

The Dragons Are Singing Tonight by Jack Prelutsky

Multicultural—

Tales the People Tell in China by Robert Wyndham

Eyes of the Dragon by Margaret Leaf

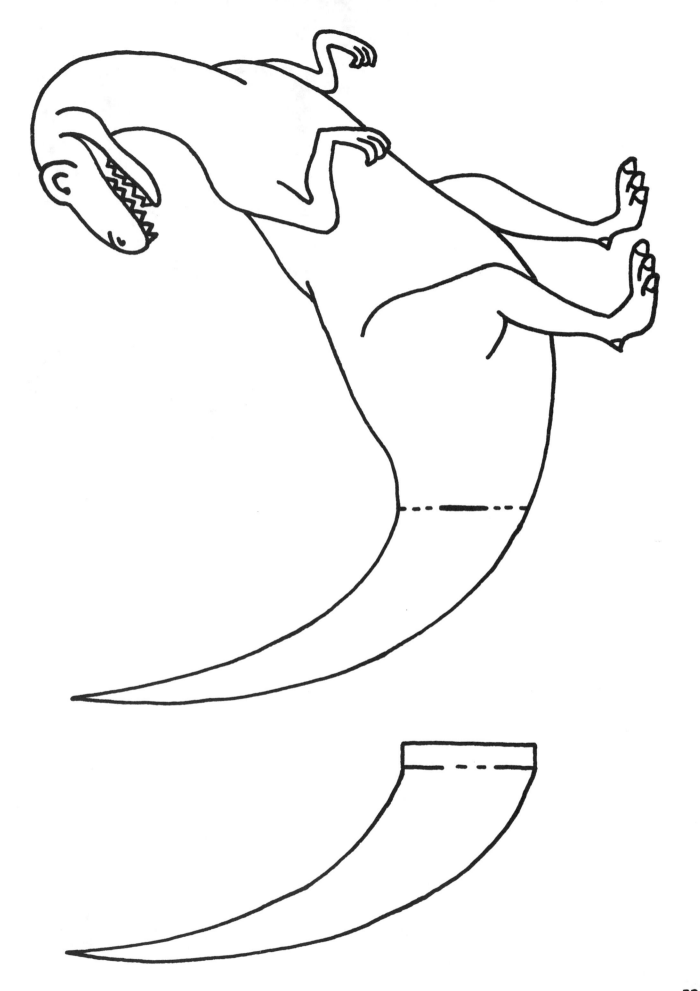

Whale

Template on page 56

A variety of whales are illustrated on the following pages. You have three options:

○ You can have your student's trace a whale by holding the tag board, with the template drawing behind it, up to a light, such as the classroom window. The whale drawing is clearly visible through the tag board, making tracing a breeze.

○ You can let the students use the illustration as a guide and draw their own whale, or

○ Students can color the template whale of their choice, cut it out and glue it to the tag board.

MATERIALS: tag board, scissors, crayons, felt-tip markers, watercolor paints or colored pencils, long-reach stapler, construction paper

1 - Fold tag board in half. With fold facing to the left, draw your whale. Have the drawing take up at least half of the cover.

2 - Color entire front cover in an underwater scene.

If you choose to have students color the

whale illustration, cut the illustration out and glue it to the cover after the underwater scene is completely colored.

3 - Cut around the top of the figure but not between the figure and the fold. This is what adds stability to the cover. Do not cut back cover.

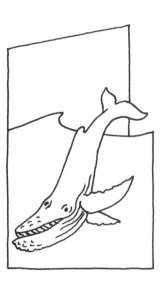

4 - Fold a piece of construction paper in half and insert into cover. Fold 8 1/2-by-11-inch sheets of paper in half and insert as pages. Staple along crease to complete.

Literature

Great Whales, The Gentle Giants by Patricia Lauber

Good Morning Whale by Achim Broger

Whale Song by Tony Johnston

Amos and Boris by William Steig

Humphrey: The Lost Whale by Wendy Tokuda.

Content Area Tie-ins

Science— endangered species, ocean life, environmental studies, whaling

Life in the Oceans by Norbert Wu

The Illustrated World of Oceans by Susan Wells

I Can Read About Whales and Dolphins by J. I. Anderson

The Sea World Book of Whales by Eve Bunting

Inside the Whale and Other Animals by Ted Dewan

Whales of the World by June Behrens

Whaling Days by Carol Carrick

Whales and Dolphins by Elizabeth Strachen

Multicultural studies—

Whale in the Sky by Anne Siberell

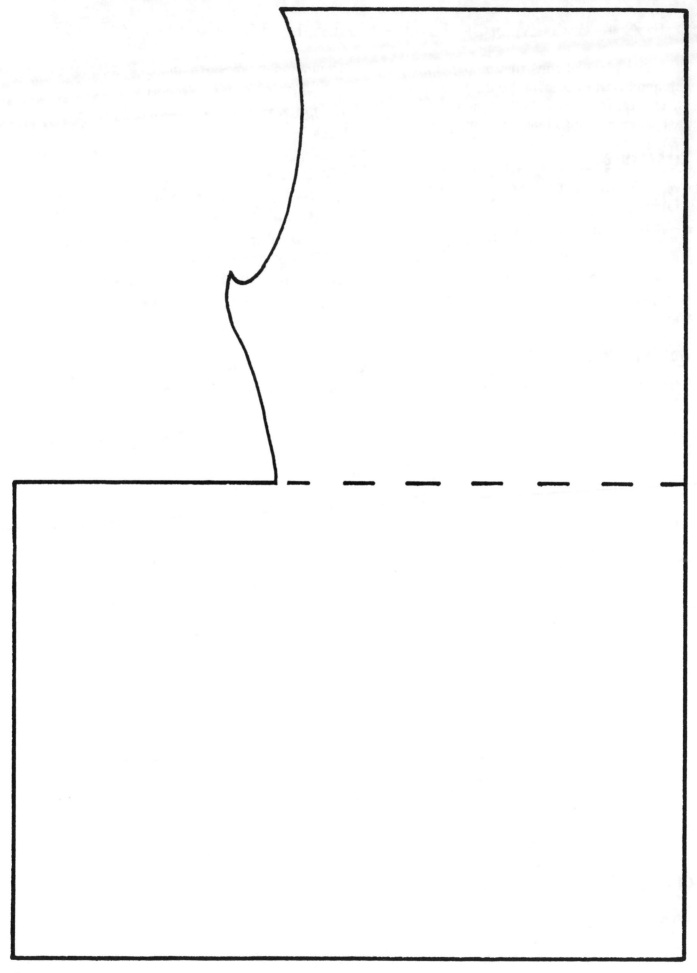

Minibooks

MINIBOOKS

The minibook is a workhorse among books. You will find hundreds of uses for it. Teachers I know use this technique for weekly homework pads, minibook reports, outlining chapters, letter books for the alphabet, riddle books, and joke books—and in short, a small, easy-to-make book fits the bill.

One class of third graders I know makes these books, without adult assistance, whenever the creative "urge to write" strikes.

MATERIALS: a 9-by-18-inch sheet of paper, crayons or felt-tip markers, scissors

DIRECTIONS:

1 - Fold the long ends of paper to meet. Crease well and unfold.

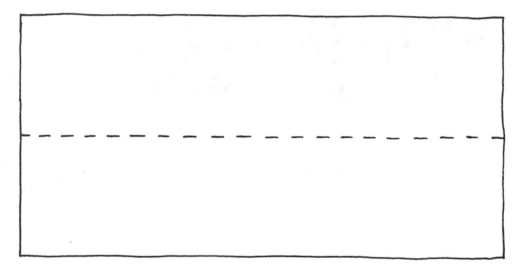

2 - Fold the right edge to meet the left edge. Crease well. Do not unfold.

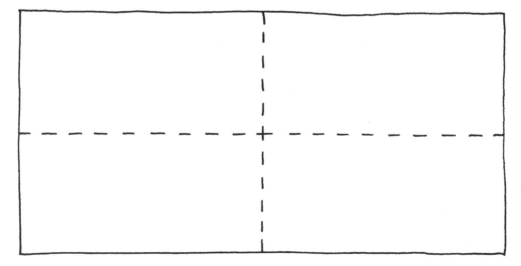

3 - Fold the right side over to meet the left side. Crease well.

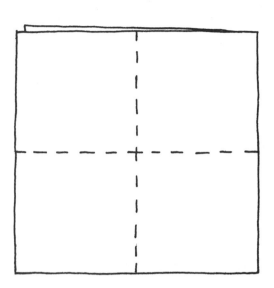 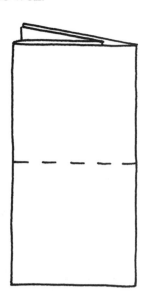

4 - Unfold the last fold.

5 - Cut on the fold along the center crease until you meet the first vertical crease.

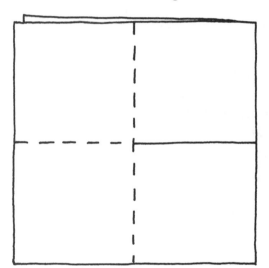 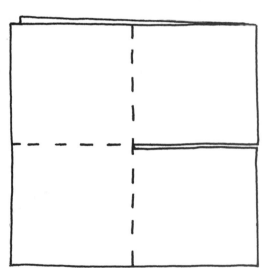

6 - Unfold.

7 - The opened page will have eight creased sections. Fold the long ends to meet as in Step One.

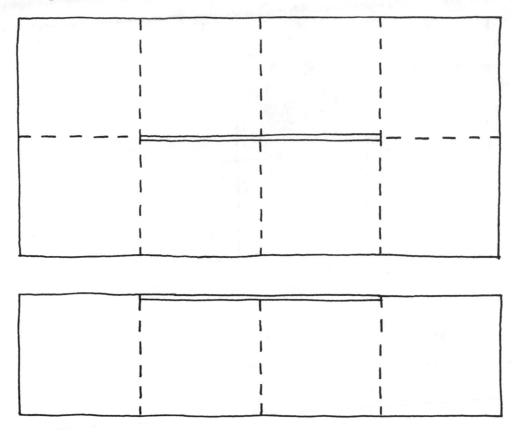

8 - Hold onto the side edges and gently push the paper inward to form a book.

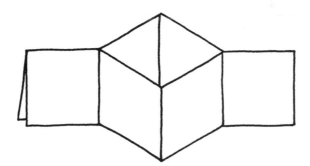

Ideas and Options

○ This book is simple to make and has dozens of uses, from creative stories to literature summaries to homework notebooks.

MAGICAL BOOKS

There is something irresistible about a tiny book that fits in the palm of your hand. And there's something magical about the way the star and flower books transform little unpretentious squares into enchanting works of art.

These charming books get the "ohs-and-ahs" whenever they are shown. Everyone wants to make one—and then everyone wants to make another one!

Star Book

MATERIALS: five pieces of construction paper, 3 3/4 inches square. Two squares of lightweight cardboard (or illustration board) for cover that are 2 inches square, two pieces of gold or silver foil wrapping paper 3 inches square, 16 inches of narrow ribbon, scissors, glue

DIRECTIONS:

1 - Fold square of paper in half horizontally and then fold it in half vertically to create a 1 3/4-inch square. Crease well.

2 - Unfold.

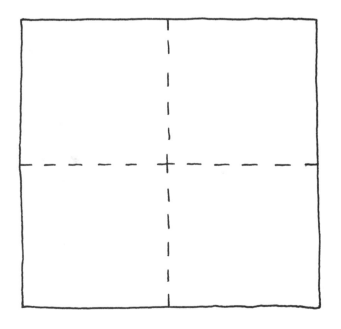

3 - Diagonally fold two opposite points of the square to meet, creating a triangle. Crease well and unfold.

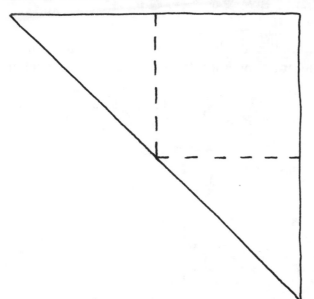

5 - Working from the center, gently bring the diagonal creases up to meet. See illustration.

Press together. The paper folds up into a 1 3/4-inch square on the outside but, when opened, reveals two triangles whose points meet in the middle. Keep paper folded.

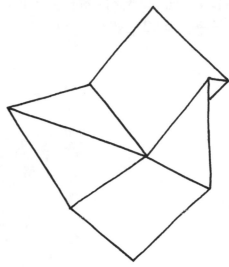

4 - Place on the table so that the diagonal crease runs horizontally.

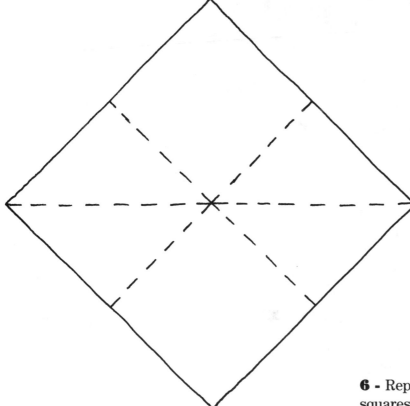

6 - Repeat steps 1 to 5 with four other squares of paper.

7 - Glue the outside of each folded square to another, back-to-back, making sure the opening point faces the upper right corner. Let dry.

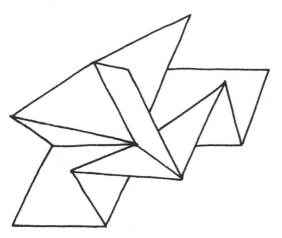

8 - Cover the two square illustration board pieces with the two 3-inch squares of gold or silver foil wrapping paper glued in place. Miter the inside corners. (See page 9 for how to miter corners).

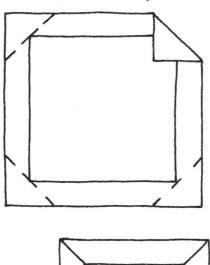

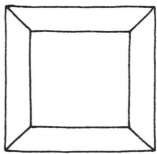

9 - Place the two cover squares, good side down, on a corner point side-by-side, tips touching.

Glue ribbon horizontally across both squares.

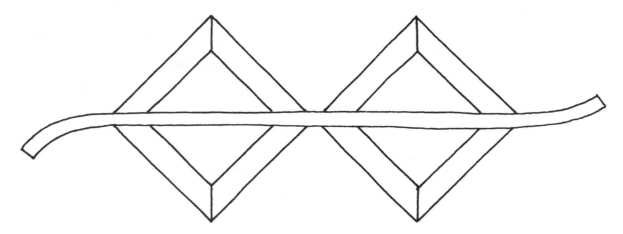

10 - The paper squares will open accordion style once they are dry. Glue the outer square fold of the paper squares to the cover squares making sure that the folded section backs inward to where the ribbon connects both cover pieces. The opening of the paper squares and the loose ribbons will all be facing the same direction.

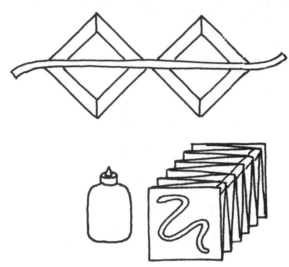

11 - Decorate and hang as an ornament.

Ideas and Options

Great as a gift, a wish book, or a little present to say "you are a light in my life." It is large enough for a little story or to write wishes. The writing is best done before the squares are folded.

Literature

Watch the Stars Come Out by Riki Levinson
Good-bye My Wishing Star by Vicki Grove
The Forgotten Door by Alexander Key

Content Area Tie-ins

Science— constellations, astrology, the solar system.

> *A Book About Planets and Stars* by Betty Polisar Reigot
>
> *Shooting Stars* by Franklyn M. Branley
>
> *The Big Dipper* by Franklyn M. Branley

Writing— The star is big enough for a student to write a short story on (before the squares are folded into shape).

Nursery Rhymes— It is suitable as an accompaniment to nursery rhymes such as "Twinkle, Twinkle, Little Star."

> *Twinkle, Twinkle Little Star* by Jane Taylor

Holidays— It could be used with Christmas stories relating to the star of Bethlehem, or with such books as:

> *Star Mother's Youngest Child* by Louise Moeri
>
> *The Christmas Sky* by Franklyn M. Branley
>
> *For Every Child A Star: A Christmas Story* by Thomas Yeomans

It is a lovely gift, or Christmas ornament.

Multicultural studies—

> *Star Boy* by Paul Goble
>
> *The Star Maiden* by Barbara Juster Esbensen
>
> *The Drinking Gourd* by F.N. Monjo

Mythology—

> *Follow the Drinking Gourd* by Jeanette Winter
>
> *D'Aulaires' Book of Greek Myths* by Ingri and Edgar P. D'Aulaire

Math— The star could be used to work with shapes, fractions, symmetry, patterns.

Flower Book

MATERIALS: six pieces of brightly colored paper, 3 3/4 inches square, two pieces of lightweight cardboard or illustration board for cover that are 2 inches square, two 3 3/4-inch squares of gold or silver foil wrapping paper, 16 inches of narrow ribbon, scissors, glue

DIRECTIONS:

Follow first seven steps as for Star Book. Then:

8 - Cut through the entire thickness of the joined-together squares to round off only the opening point of the squares. Do not cut into the other three folds.* See illustration.

9 - Cover the two square illustration board pieces with two 3 3/4-inch squares of gold or silver foil wrapping paper. Glue in place. Miter the inside corners. See page 9 for how-to.

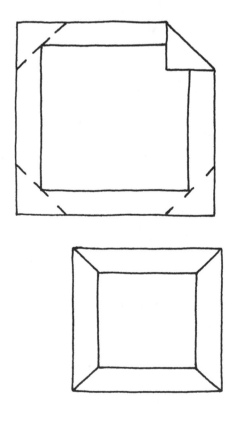

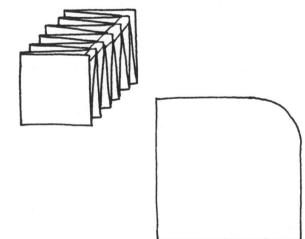

10 - Place the two cover squares on a point side-by-side, tips touching. Glue ribbon horizontally across both squares.

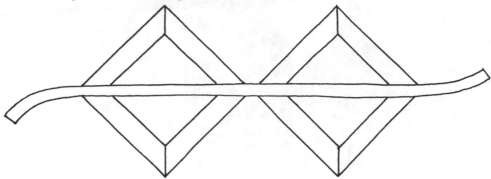

11 - Once dry the paper squares will open accordion style. Glue the outer fold of the paper accordion to the cover squares, making sure that the folded section backs inward to where the ribbon connects both cover pieces. The opening of the paper squares and the loose ribbons will all be facing the same direction. Let dry; then open to reveal a lovely flower.

* This step rewards experimentation: As long as you cut between the creases on either side of the opening point, you will create a flower. The cut can be symmetrical, wavy, or jagged. It will form the petals of a wide variety of flowers.

Literature

Wild Wild Sunflower Child Anna by Nancy White Calstrom

The Reason for a Flower by Ruth Heller

A Seed Is a Promise by Claire Merrill

Flowers by Rena K. Kirkpatrick

Plant Families by Carol Lerner

Content Area Tie-ins

Science— This flower could be used rather dramatically with the study of plant life by drawing a seed on the cover and opening it into a flower. Eliminate Step 9 if you plan to draw on the cover.

Holidays/Gifts— This minibook is a great gift and totally surprises anyone who opens the little square to find a blossoming flower. Suitable for celebrations of spring, Earth Day, Caregiver's Day, Grandparents' Day, etc.

Folding Books

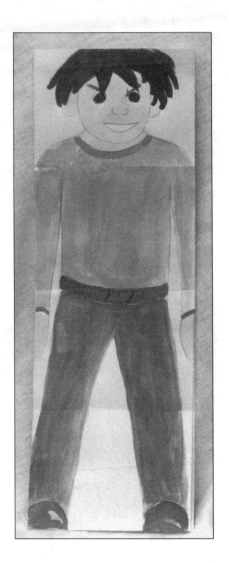

UNFOLDING BOOKS

This is a tidy little book, easy to make in a small work area. Designed from a single sheet of large paper and folded just right to open—and open and open, this book can be made by even very young children.

There are either two or three pages for writing and an area for a long illustration which makes it ideal for an alligator book, a dinosaur, a panoramic view, or (if the paper is held vertically) something tall like a giant or a skyscraper!

The directions for an unfolding book are the same, regardless of how you decide to use it. In our example, we will make an alligator.

The second type of unfolding book is larger (9 by 12 inches when closed) and involves taping three pieces of tag board together at the sides. It is a great size for reports, and fun because the outside cover is a shape. In the example (page 72) a human body is made for a report on how the body works. This book stands very well, gives a nice presentation and can take many different shapes! It can, for example, be a ship, a jar containing an experiment (how beans form roots), or perhaps a box with hints given on what is inside as you open the pages.

Alligator/Crocodile

Template on page 71
MATERIALS: one sheet of 11-by-18-inch white paper, crayons or felt-tip markers

DIRECTIONS:

1 - Fold paper in half as in illustration.

2 - Fold paper in half and half again creating four equal panels..

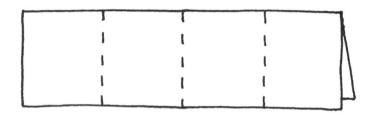

3 - Open the paper to view the creases. Fold the right edge to the first crease and then again to the next crease.

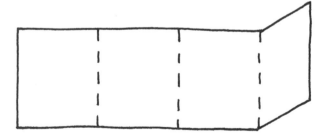

4 - Bring the left side panel over the other folded sections. This is the cover of the book.

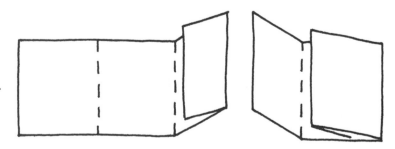

5 - Open the cover. Writing will be done on the right side panel. Unfold this panel and write again on the right side panel. Unfold again and write for the third time on the right side panel. The illustration is done on the three left panels. (See illustrations on page 70.)

The way this book is made, as you read the written work and turn a page, more and more of the illustration is revealed. For just two pages of written work, the illustration can extend from side to side across the four inside panels.

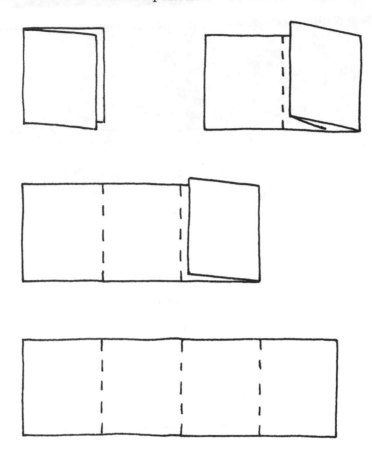

6 - Complete illustration.

Literature and Content Area Tie-ins

Endangered Species—

Never Kiss an Alligator! by Colleen Stanley Bare

Lyle, Lyle Crocodile by Bernard Waber

Crocodarling by Mary Rayner

The Enormous Crocodile by Roald Dahl

Ideas and Options

○ By turning the page the other way, you can draw a giant.

Abiyoyo by Pete Seeger

The Boy and the Giants by Fiona Moodie

The Selfish Giant by Oscar Wilde

○ Other possibilities you can draw include a lovely landscape set in a particular time period from prehistoric times to a Native American village. Or you can draw the community you live in, the school you go to, or a place you visited on a field trip.

○ Long dinosaurs are another choice, as are long creatures like snakes, lizards or even whales. Read *Giants of Land, Sea and Air: Past and Present* by David Peters.

○ If your class is studying fractions, a math lesson can be incorporated into the making of the book. The large sheet of paper is divided into eighths and then halved, and so on.

○ You could also draw the same tree on all four panels showing the change of seasons.

Human

Template on page 74

MATERIALS: three pieces of tag board, scissors, crayons, cloth tape, white writing paper

DIRECTIONS:

1 - Copy template design on three pieces of tag board and cut figure out from the elbows up.

2 - Take the top piece of tag board and turn it over to the left. Take the second piece of tag board and turn it over to the right. Tape the pieces together. The objective is to align the three pieces so when the book is closed the human forms line up precisely.

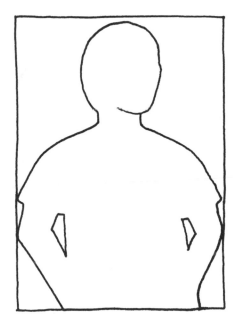

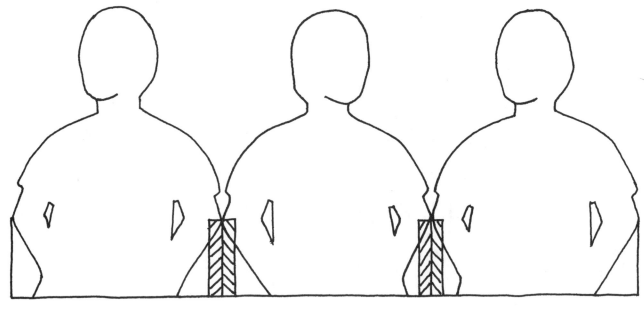

3 - Close the book up. The left side panel is the cover. When opened, the left side panel has the title and author, and the right panel of tag board, in this case, has a drawing of internal organs which can be labeled for the report. This page could also be used for written work.

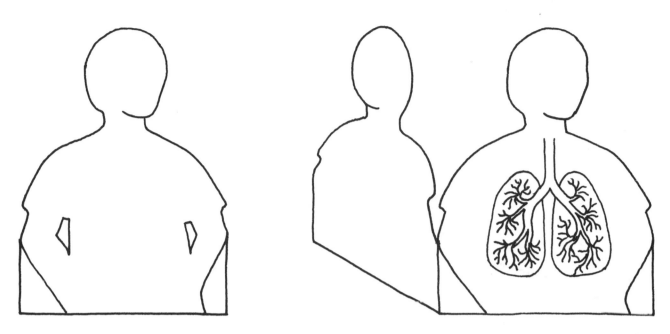

4 - The right side page is then opened to reveal two clear pages for writing. A second choice would be to fold several sheets of 8 1/2-by-11-inch paper in half and staple the written report to the back page. White 8 1/2 by 11 paper will need to be trimmed slightly to fit.

5 - Color to complete. The entire book will stand nicely for display if opened into a triangle.

Literature

Blood and Guts, A Working Guide to Your Own Insides by Linda Allison

How Your Body Works by Judy Hindley and Colin King

The Human Body by Jonathan Miller

The Human Body by Mary Elting

Ideas and Options

○ As long as the bottom of the page remains level, this type of book could be made for any subject. For example, a frog could be drawn on the cover and its internal organs could be shown on the inside cover.

○ Other possibilities are a house, ship or castle. In these cases, showing the interior could be the report itself.

○ The book could be made into a character from a folk or fairy tale or a myth.

○ It could also be a book about the student. In this case you would have the student do a self-portrait on one sheet of tag board and trace it onto the two other pieces of tag board. It would make a nice presentation for open house and samples of the student's work could be tucked inside.

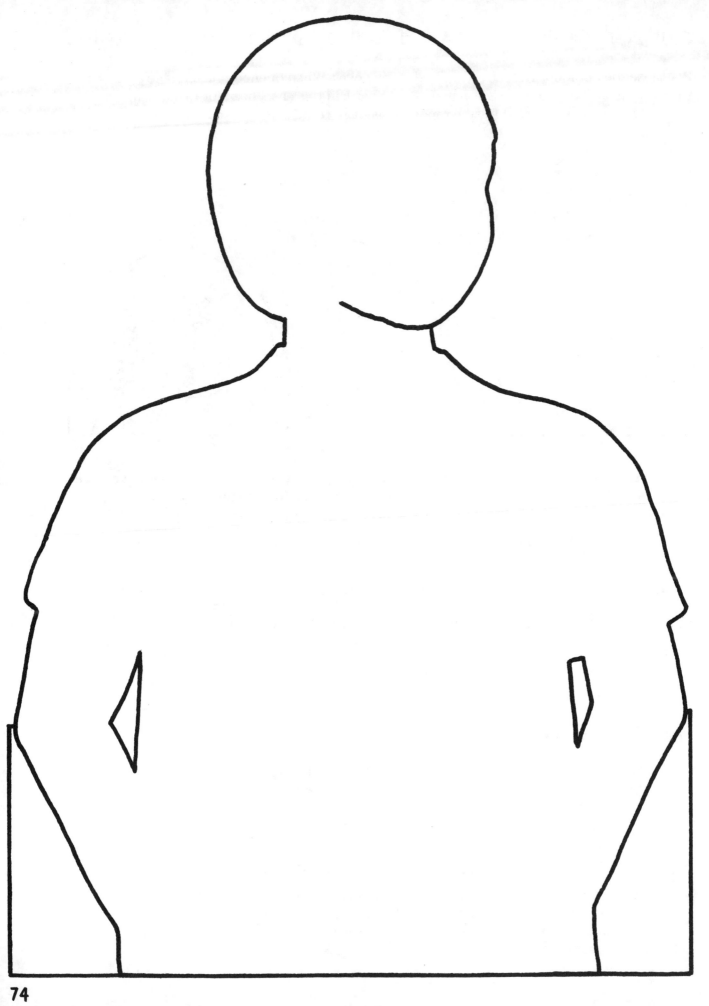

FLAP BOOKS

From the youngest child to the oldest adult, no one can resist the surprise of a flap book. The charm is in not knowing what is under the flap. Our curiosity gets the best of us and we must take a peek.

Children enjoy these books, even if they're the creators and know the surprise! And they love sharing these books with their classmates, giggling with anticipation as the other person gets ready to lift the flap.

Directions are given for a door, a house/storefront, and a leaf: let your imagination provide you with other ideas for more doors!

Door

Patterns for front door or closet door on page 77

MATERIALS: tag board, utility knife, pencil, glue, crayons, felt-tip markers or colored pencils

DIRECTIONS:

1 - Fold one piece of tag board in half and crease well. Decide the door shape, size and location on either half of the page but not along the center crease.

2 - Draw the door or use the patterns.

3 - Cut along the top edge, the side with the door handle and the bottom edge of the door with a utility knife. Gently crease the door along the remaining side, creating the flap.

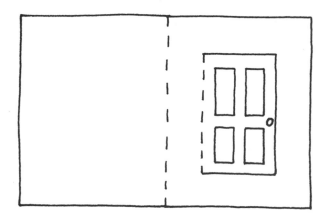

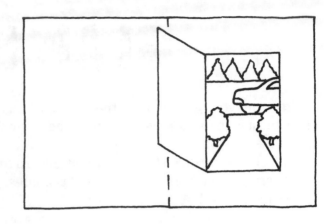

4 - Complete drawing. Be sure to color both sides of the door.

5 - Place piece of white construction paper behind door opening and mark the door outline. This will indicate where you should draw the behind-the-door scene after you take the door away.

6 - Completely color the behind-the-door scene. Then line up the drawing and glue the scene in place by putting a small amount of glue around the door edges.

Ideas and Options

○ Open House: Take a photograph of each student and measure the door opening to be 1/4 smaller all around than the photograph. Cut the door opening on three sides with a utility knife. Let each student draw their school around the door opening. Glue the photo in place behind the door and use as a "Welcome to My School" folder for parent's conference day or open house.

○ The door can be used as one illustration in a larger pop-up book by using back-to-back construction.

Literature and Content Area Tie-Ins:

Door-

There's a Nightmare in My Closet by Mercer Mayer

The Hundred Dresses by Eleanor Estes

Red Riding Hood by James Marshall

The Secret Garden by Frances Hodgson Burnett

The Forgotten Door by Alexander Key

Tollbooth Door—

The Phantom Tollbooth by Norton Juster

Cupboard—

The Indian in the Cupboard by Lynne Reid Banks

Old Mother Hubbard. The Real Mother Goose illustrated by Blanche F. Wright

Multicultural—

The Lily Cupboard by Shulamith Oppenheim

Teaching Resoures—

25 Thematic Mini-Books by Deborah Kovacs

25 Mother Goose Peek-a-Books by Helen H. Moore

25 Science Mini-Books by Esther Weiner

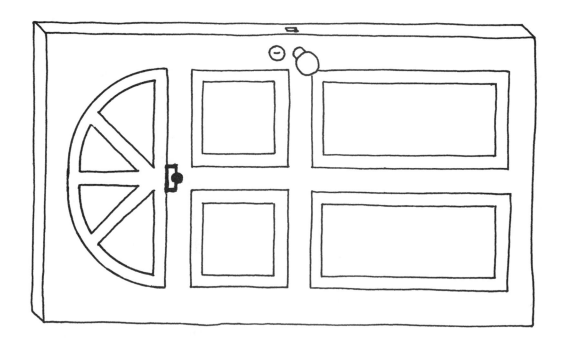

House/Storefront

Template on page 80

MATERIALS: two pieces of tag board, ruler, clear tape, scissors, crayons, stapler

DIRECTIONS:

1 - Draw a large house on one piece of tag board or use template on page 80. Without the template, students can draw their own home, a particular store in their town, or their grandparents' home.

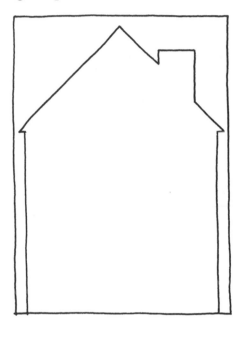

2 - Color house and cut it out.

3 - If you anticipate that the written work will be lengthy, create a strip-hinge on left side of house by cutting a 1/2 inch strip up the left side. Reattach the strip with tape, leaving 1/16 inch between the strip and the rest of the house.

If the written work is less than four pages, you can staple the work to the back cover.

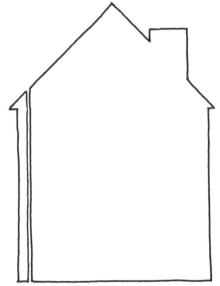

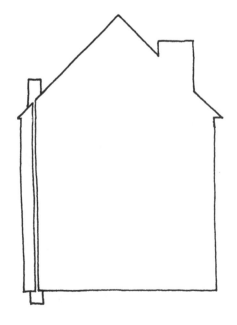

4 - Trace the house on paper that will be the inside pages of the book and cut out.

5 - Staple the cover and the inside pages and to the full piece of tag board.

6 - On the first inside page, you might choose to let the students draw the inside of their house, including furnishings, people and pets. Another possibility is to draw the interior of a store showing what goods or services are purchased there.

Literature and Content Area Tie-ins

Houses by Piero Ventura

The New House by Joyce Maynard

Building a House by Byron Barton

The Little House by Virginia Lee Burton

A House Is a House for Me by Mary Ann Hoberman

Need a House? Call Mrs. Mouse by George Mendoza

Content Area Tie-ins

Community—

Where the Children Live by Thomas B. Allen

All About Things People Do by Melanie and Chris Rice

American History— colonial house, log cabin, schoolhouse

If you Lived in Colonial Times by Ann McGovern

Lincoln: A Photobiography by Russell Freedman

Little House on the Prairie by Laura Ingalls Wilder

Log Cabin in the Woods—

A True Story about a Pioneer Boy by Joanne L. Henry

Visiting a Village by Bobbie Kalman

Multicultural Studies—

The Village of Round and Square Houses by Ann Grifalconi

Nursery Rhymes/Fairy Tales—

Any story with a house, including the *Three Little Pigs, Goldilocks, Little Red Riding Hood, Hansel and Gretel.*

Leaf Flap

Template on page 83

MATERIALS: two pieces of tag board, glue, scissors, crayons.

DIRECTIONS:

1 - Fold one piece of tag board in half and set aside. This forms the cover of the book. The illustration will be made on the right side of the page; the written work will be on the left side.

2 - On another piece of tag board draw a leaf. It can be any type of leaf, from a bean leaf for Jack and the Beanstalk to a cabbage leaf in a garden that hides a small rabbit, or the leaf of a mighty oak hiding a squirrel. Template for various leaves on page 83.

3 - Cut leaf out. If you draw your own leaf, make sure the leaf is large enough to hide whatever you intend to draw behind it. If not, draw two leaves together and cut them out.

4 - Completely color the front and back of the leaf.

5 - Crease a strip about 1/2 inch width along the left side of the leaf. Glue this edge on the right side of the folded piece of tag board, which is where the illustration will be.

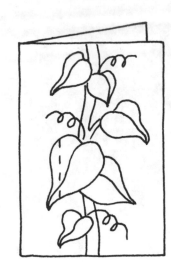

6 - Draw and color the plant and whatever is behind the flap.

Literature and Content Area Tie-ins

Nursery Rhymes—

Jack and the Beanstalk or *Little Bo Peep* (The sheep might be hiding behind a bush).

Jack and the Bean Tree by Gail E. Haley

Jim and the Beanstalk by Raymond Briggs

The Real Mother Goose illustrated by Blanche F. Wright

Science— plant life. The inside of the flap could label the parts of the leaf.

Tree species— You could make a book where different leaf species are made into flaps with the name of the species under the flap.

Leaves by Rena K. Kirkpatrick

Trees and Leaves by Rosie Harlow and Gareth Morgan

All About Trees by Jane Dickinson

Insects— Insects that consume a particular plant could be drawn and labelled.

Dinosaurs— Draw a dense forest and have a flap conceal the head of a Tyrannosaurus Rex.

Tyrannosaurus Was a Beast by Jack Prelutsky

Endangered species— Rainforest animals could be hidden behind the huge leaf of a jungle plant.

Rainforest Animals by Michael Chinery

Rainforest by Helen Cowcher

POP-UP BOOKS

Pop-ups are just pure fun. They are easy to do and give a lot of thrill for the effort.

The pop-up designs that follow can be used individually as single illustrations in a story or used together to make a pop-up book. With the latter idea, think of the individual pop-ups as part of a complete story.

For example, with a creative story, the mouth pop-up could be the character speaking. The house pop-up could be the setting of the story. The face could be a close-up of a character, and so on.

These pop-ups also make great reports. The words for the report can be written on the same page as the pop-ups, or using back-to-back construction; a page of written work can be added as often as every other page. You can accomplish this in different ways:

1 - Use horizontally lined 8 1/2-by-11-inch sheets of paper folded in half. Students can write their assignment directly on the paper which is then inserted as above.

2 - Use regular paper and cut it into 6-by-9-inch rectangles which can be glued onto tag board and then into the book using back-to-back construction.

3 - Have students write directly on the pop-up page.

For math, pop-ups can be used to reinforce shapes. Using the examples that follow you can make triangles, squares, rectangles and circles.

Still another possibility for pop-ups are cards for celebrations or holidays:

❍ The mouth could say any sentiment from "Happy Birthday" to Bon Voyage."

❍ The face could throw a kiss for Valentine's Day.

❍ The house could be "From our house to your house . . . .Merry Christmas."

The Mouth

Template on page 86

MATERIALS: crayons, felt-tip markers, watercolor paints or colored pencils, ruler, tag board, scissors, glue, construction paper

DIRECTIONS:

1 - Fold a piece of tag board in half. Crease it well. The better the crease, the better the pop-up. Place the fold to your right.

2 - About halfway down the page, draw a line 1 1/2 inches long. Cut on this line.

3 - Bend each flap back at an angle and crease well. By experimenting with the angle of the fold you will create many variations of mouths.

4 - Open the page like a mountain in front of you and push the flaps through to the other side.

The mouth is now ready to color. Is it a frog? A bird's beak?

5 - Cut a square of red or pink construction paper that is large enough to cover the back of the open mouth and glue it in place by putting a dab of glue on each of the four corners.

Ideas and Options

○ Using serrated pinking shears to cut the mouth makes rows of teeth that could suit a lion or tiger or any other creature with sharp teeth.

○ By cutting jagged lines you can make an egg cracking open.

○ You can cut fangs into the mouth as well for a horrid dragon, Count Dracula, or other beast.

Literature

Frog

Frog and Toad Are Friends by Arnold Lobel

Frog Went A-Courtin' by John Langstaff and Feodor Rojankovsky

The Candlewick Book of Fairy Tales, retold by Sara Hayes (The Frog Prince)

The Frog Prince Continued by Jon Scieszka

Bird

Are You My Mother? by P.D. Eastman

The Ugly Ducking. Hans Andersen's Fairy Tales by L.W. Kingsland

Lion

The Lion, the Witch and the Wardrobe by C.S. Lewis

The Best of Aesop's Fables, compiled by Margaret Clark

Tiger

The Jungle Book and Just So Stories by Rudyard Kipling

Nine-in-one Grr! Grr! told by Blia Xiong and adapted by Cathy Spagnoli

Cracking Egg

Egg to Chick by Millicent Selsam

Chicken Aren't the Only Ones by Ruth Heller

Content Area Tie-ins

Science— life cycle of a frog, birds, pond life, endangered species.

Frogs, Toads, Lizards and Salamanders by Nancy Winslow Parker and Joan Richards Wright

Turtles, Toads and Frogs by George Fichter

Myths— Cyclops (cut the line about 3/4 of the way up the page - forehead level)

D'Aulaires' Book of Greek Myths by Ingri and Edgar P. D'Aulaire

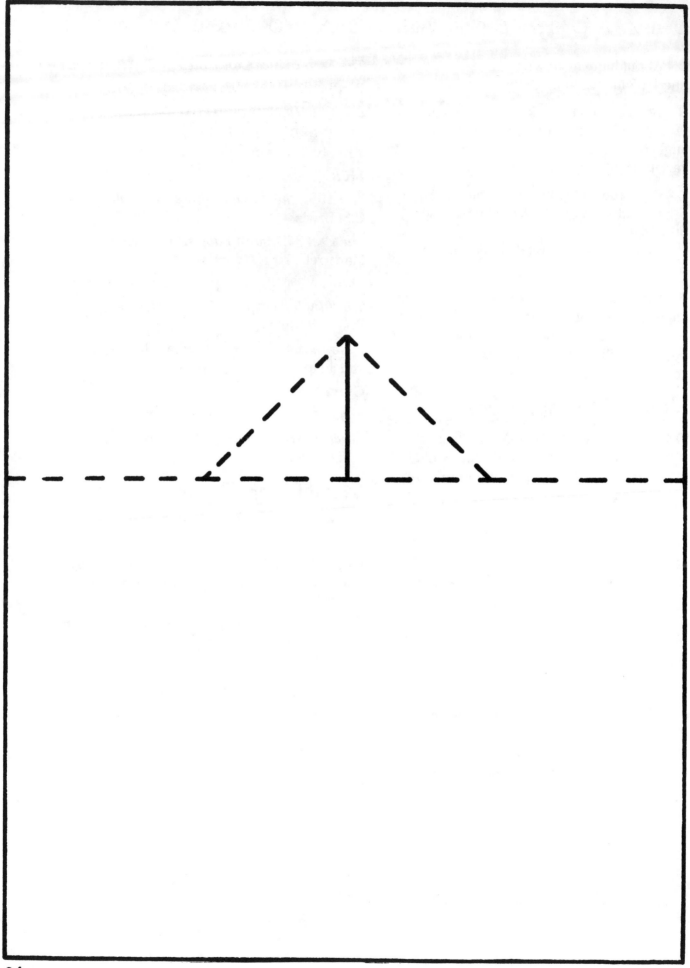

The House

Template on page 88

MATERIALS: crayons, felt-tip markers, watercolor paints or colored pencils, tag board, scissors.

DIRECTIONS:

1 - Fold a piece of tag board in half. Crease it well. Place the fold to your right.

2 - Draw the outline of half of a house, making sure the end of the roof line and the edge of the floor are in line.

3 - Cut only the roof line and the base of the house.

4 - Fold the flap back and forth until it's well-creased. Open the page like a mountain in front of you. Push the flap through to the other side.

5 - Decorate.

Literature

The Big Orange Splot by
D. Manus Pinkwater

The House on Maple Street by Bonnie Pryor

Building a House by Byron Barton

The Little House by Virginia Lee Burton

A House Is a House for Me by
Mary Ann Hoberman

Need a House? Call Ms. Mouse by
George Mendoza

Little House on the Prairie by
Laura Ingalls Wilder

Roxaboxen by Alice McLerran

Content Area Tie-ins

American history— a house from any century, any culture, any climate. Excellent for use with a report. For a report, the house pop-up could be on the front inside cover. The rest of the pages could be for the report.

Social Studies— community (store fronts), family (could be the student's house, grandparent's house, vacation house, dog house). Excellent for reports.

Multicultural studies— the homes of various cultures, past and present.

> *Where the Children Live* by
> Thomas B. Allen.

> *The Village of Round and Square Houses* by Ann Grifalconi

Math— symmetry

Creative Writing— a story character's house

Holidays—

Christmas (a gingerbread house)

Halloween (a haunted house),

Thanksgiving (family gathering).

Fairy Tales and Fables—

> *Little Red Riding Hood, Snow White, Cinderella.*

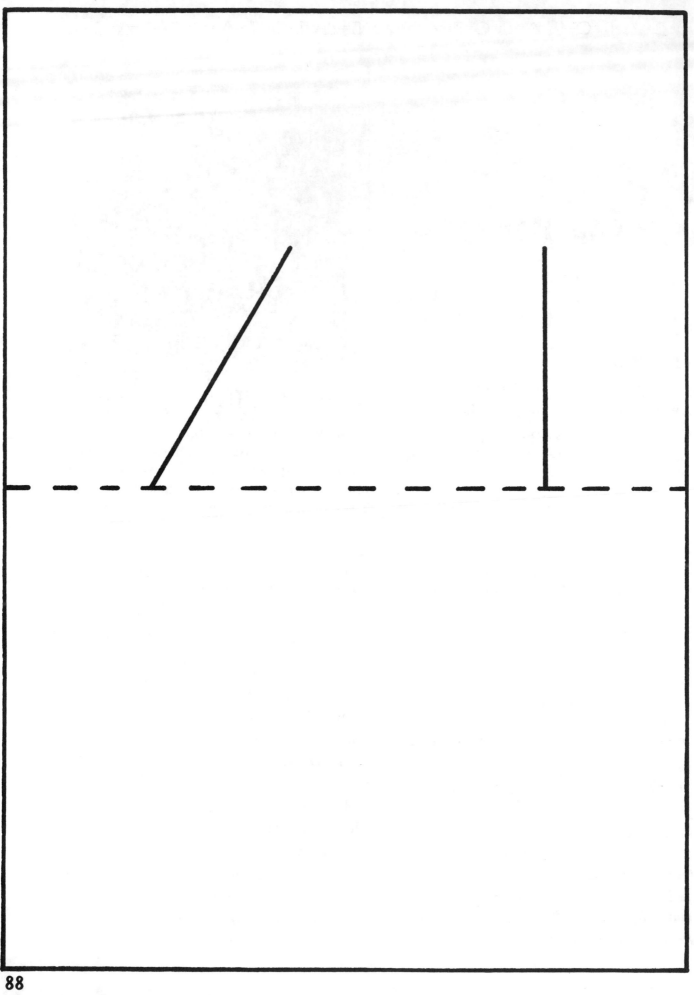

The Face

Template on page 90

MATERIALS: crayons, felt-tip markers, watercolor paints or colored pencils, tag board, scissors, glue, construction paper

DIRECTIONS:

1 - Fold a piece of tag board in half. Crease it well. Place the fold to your right.

2 - Draw half of an oval at the fold. Be sure the top and bottom edges are rounded.

3 - Halfway down the oval, draw two pencil marks 2 inches apart.

4 - Cut from the top of the oval to the top mark. Then cut from the bottom of the oval to the bottom mark.

5 - Fold the flap back and forth until it is well-creased. Open the page like a mountain in front of you. Push the flap through to the other side.

6 - Design and color. You can add "extras" such as construction paper hair, glasses, ears and earrings.

Literature and Content Area Tie-ins

Literature and Content Area Tie-ins are infinitely numerous since this face can be anyone from a princess to a pirate, a child to a old man, and everyone else on the planet. It can also be a ladybug or an egg.

Still another possibility is to draw the face to relate to a social studies unit and reinforce it with literature. For example, draw a Native American to accompany the book *Buffalo Woman* by Paul Goble and reinforce that unit of study. Or the face could be of a historical figure, say Abraham Lincoln, to commemorate his birthday. In this case, black construction paper in the shape of a stovepipe hat could be added to the face.

Be creative. All sorts of features and accessories can be added from braided pig-tails, to moustaches, to wiggly ears. Just cut them out of construction paper and add them to the face.

This same pop-up can be a globe (for earth studies), a planet (solar system), or a ball simply by drawing a half circle instead of the oval.

Math— symmetry. If drawn as an Easter egg, the symmetry could extend into the festive design on the egg.

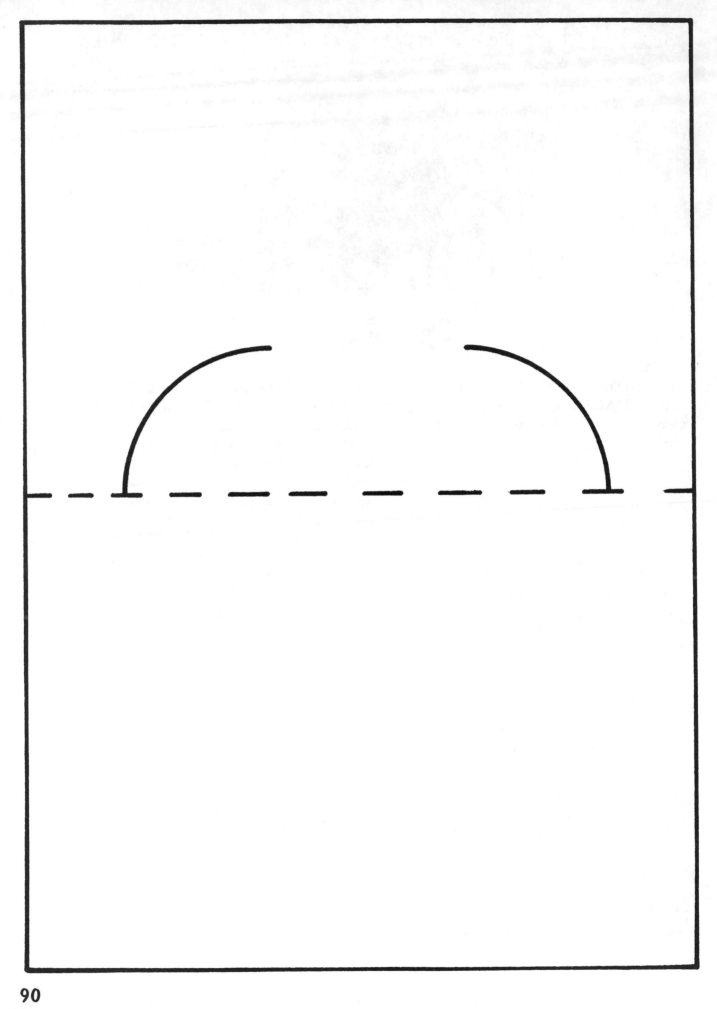

Ideas and Options

The following illustrations show the fold and cut outlines for more pop-ups:

egg, bug, cat, butterfly, fairy, leaf, tulip, planet, ball, hot-air balloon, chick, penguin, turtle, fox, sun, moon, ship, heart, froglet, knight's helmet, teepee, pumpkin, dreidel, flying saucer, owl, and umbrella.

Literature

Egg
Rechenka's Eggs by Patricia Polacco
Marushka's Egg by Elsa Okon Rael
The Enormous Egg by Oliver Butterworth
Chickens Aren't the Only Ones by Ruth Heller

Butterfly/Fairy
Butterflies and Moths by George Fichter
The Real Tooth Fairy by Marilyn Kaye

Turtle
Turtles, Toads and Frogs by George Fichter

Umbrella
Umbrella by Taro Yashima
The Yellow Umbrella by Henrik Drescher
The Enchanted Umbrella by Odette Meyers

Fox
Fables by Arnold Lobel
Flossie and the Fox by Patricia McKissack
The Best of Aesop's Fable compiled by Margaret Clark

Cat
Puss 'N Boots. The Candlewick Book of Fairy Tales retold by Sarah Hayes
The Owl and the Pussycat by Edward Lear and Jan Brett

Owl
Good-Night Owl! by Pat Hutchins
Owl Moon by Jane Yolen
The Owl and the Pussycat by Edward Lear and Jan Brett

Hot-Air Balloon
The Great Round-the-World Balloon Race by Sue Scullard
The Big Balloon Race by Eleanor Coerr

Pumpkin
The Biggest Pumpkin Ever by Steven Kroll
Pumpkin, Pumpkin by Jeanne Titherington

Earth/Globe/Sun/Moon/Planets
Keepers of the Earth by Michael J. Caduto and Joseph Bruchac
Earth Day by Linda Lowery

Snowman
The Snowman by Raymond Briggs
The Black Snowman by Phil Mendez

Leaf/Bugs
Bugs by Nancy W. Parker and Joan R. Wright
The Grouchy Ladybug by Eric Carle

Teepee
Teepee Tales of the American Indian by Dee Brown
The Tipi: A Center of Native American Life by David Charlotte Yue

Ship— Could be used for Columbus Day or Thanksgiving
How Many Days to America? by Eve Bunting
Where Do You Think You're Going Christopher Columbus? by Jean Fritz

Chick
From Egg to Chick by Millicent Selsam
Chickens by Lynn Stone

Penguin
Mr. Popper's Penguin's by Richard and Florence Atwater
Penguins by Norman Barrett

Knight's helmet— Any of the legends of King Arthur.
Medieval Knights by Trevor Cairns

Fish
In the Pond by Ermanno Cristini and Luigi Puricelli

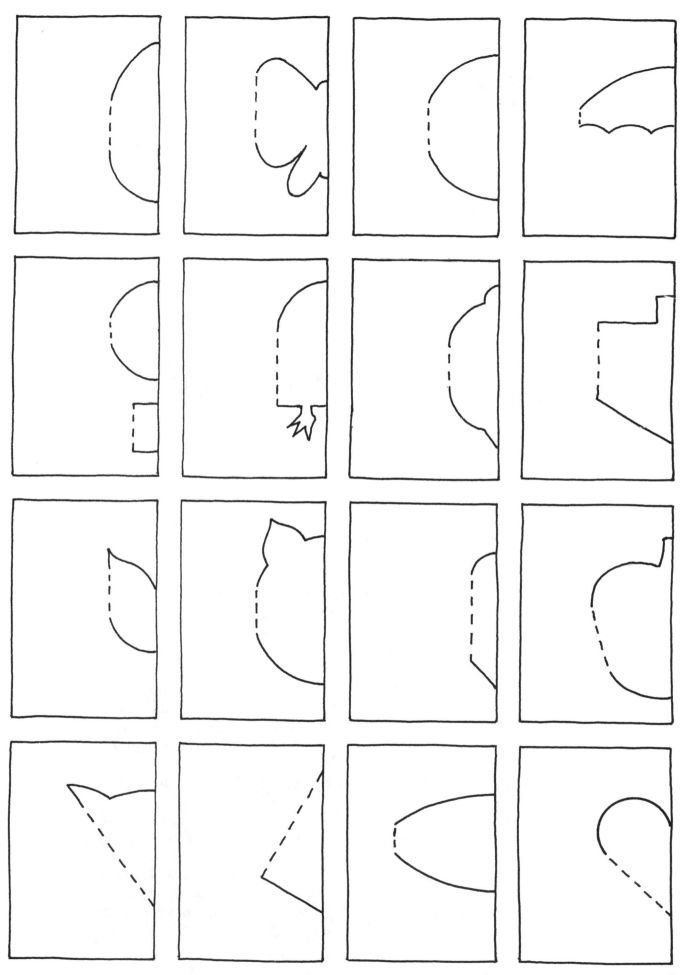

CUT-ANGLE BOOKS

A book where the pages are all cut angles offers surprise after surprise for the reader. As each page is turned, another pop-up jumps up to greet you. For the book's author knowing what comes next doesn't seem to detract from the fun. Another nice feature of this book is its size; smaller than most, it fits nicely into child-size hands.

The directions that follow are for the mouse. However, the first five steps explain the general technique that you can use to make any cut-angle pop-up.

To make a cut-angle book, use back-to-back construction. Otherwise, cover the finished cut angle illustration with a 6-by-12-inch piece of construction paper.

A third grade child used cut angles in a report about the lifecycle of a tree. He started the report with a cut angle of a hefty full grown tree with a woodpecker making a hole in the trunk; the next page showed the trunk close-up. The student used a stand that ran the length of the page to show the trunk and a hole punch to make dozens of holes in the bark.

The third page showed the tree falling down. To accomplish this, the student drew the trunk on a separate piece of tag board, cut it out and used a brad to attach the trunk to the bottom of the page. This way, the trunk could be pull to the right and fall to the ground.

The fourth page was a drawing of the trunk rotting on the ground and little animals making their homes inside.

The fifth page was another cut angle, smaller than the first, depicting a new tree growing in the same spot.

On each page, the student had written a few sentences explaining the life of a tree.

If your class is writing more than a few sentences per page, cut as many 6-by-12-inch rectangles out of tag board each student will need and either have student write directly on the tag board or use lined paper and glue sheets of the lined pages onto the tag board rectangles which will give students guidelines for their written work. These pages are incorporated, with the book's illustrations, in a book using back-to-back construction.

Mouse

Templates on pages 97–98 (Template of page 97 is for mouse, page 98 is a generic pop-up.)

MATERIALS: crayons, felt-tip markers, watercolor paints or colored pencils, tag board, ruler and scissors

DIRECTIONS:

1 - Fold tag board in half.

2 - With the opening to the right, fold the top left corner down until it meets the right side. Crease well.

3 - Measure up from the bottom 6 inches and draw a line. Cut off tag board above this line.

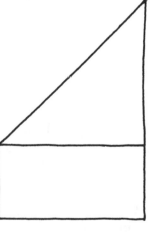

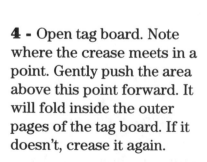

4 - Open tag board. Note where the crease meets in a point. Gently push the area above this point forward. It will fold inside the outer pages of the tag board. If it doesn't, crease it again.

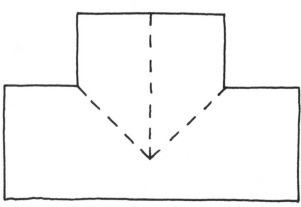

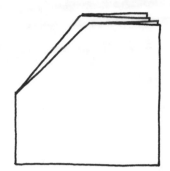

5 - Open the tag board again. The middle section will pop up as the page is opened.

6 - Draw the head of the mouse in the section that pops up.

7 - If you have your students draw their own mouse, be sure they fill the pop-up section with their drawing. After the coloring is complete, you may decide to trim around the drawing, as in the photograph of the mouse. When cutting around the figure, do not cut down into the angle. It will weaken the pop-up. Instead cut straight across from the 6-inch measurement line.

8 - A book of six to eight cut-angle pages can be constructed using the back-to-back construction technique shown on page 10.

Ideas and Options

○ Although the example above is a mouse, this cut-angle can be a lion, a crab, a shark, a dog, a cat or any other animal.

○ If you want to be really creative, turn the cut angle upside down! Now the pop-up portion seems to pour from the bottom. It could be letters spilling out from a mail bag, water flowing from a jug, or the wing of a bird that sweeps up and down with the movement of the page.

Literature

Mouse

If You Give a Mouse a Cookie by Laura Jaffe Numeroff

The Best of Aesop's Fables compiled by Margaret Clark (The Cat and the Mice, The Lion and the Mouse, Town Mouse City Mouse)

Fables by Arnold Lobel

Julius, the Baby of the World by Kevin Henkes

The Tale of Two Bad Mice by Beatrix Potter

The Tale of Johnny Town-Mouse by Beatrix Potter

Oscar the Mouse Finds a Home by Moria Miller and Maria Majewska

The Story of Jumping Mouse by John Steptoe

The Church Mouse by Graham Oakley

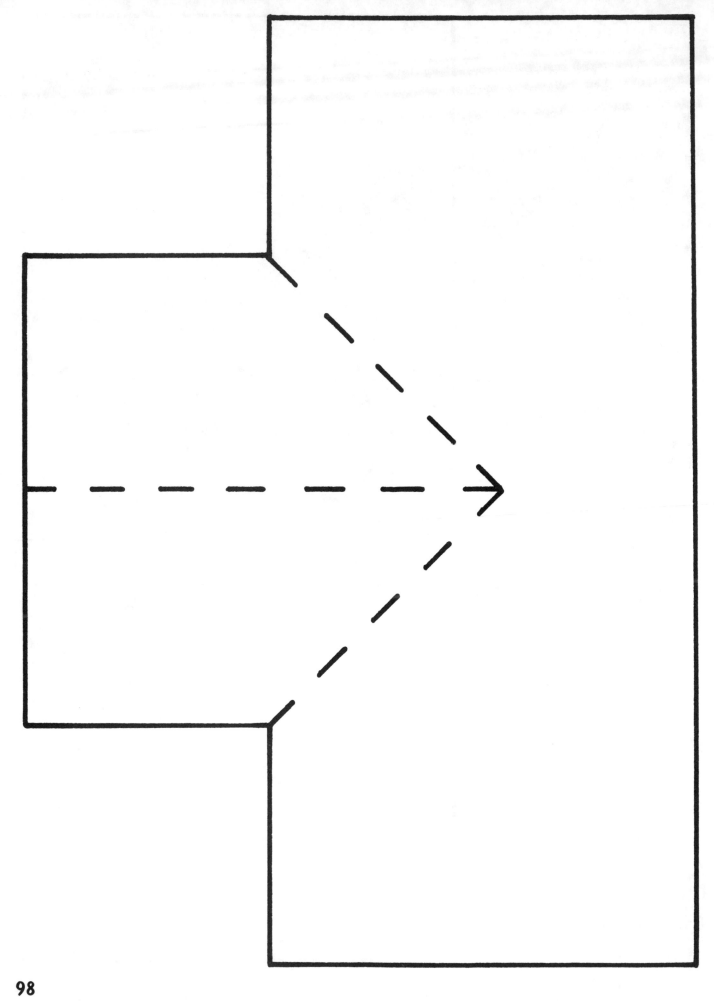

VALENTINE HEART: The cut angle technique makes a great card. With a little special trimming it can be a heart for Valentine's Day, a bouquet of flowers for any occasion or a turkey for thanksgiving. See directions that follow.

Valentine Heart

Template on page 100

To make the heart, follow directions 1 through 5 on pages 95–96. Fold the card in half and on the upper portion, draw the top of a heart. Let the angle crease be the bottom portion of the heart.

6 - Cut out only the top of the heart. (See template.)

7 - Open the tag board and gently push the upper part of the heart in toward the center. Close and crease well. When the page is opened, the heart will pop-up.

8 - Color the Valentine card. Glue a 6-by-12-inch piece of red construction paper to the outside of the card, being careful not to glue near the pop-up.

Literature

Somebody Loves You, Mr. Hatch by Eileen Spinelli

Secret Valentine by Catherine Stock

It's Valentine's Day by Jack Prelutsky

Ideas and Options

The upside-down cut-angle heart looks like a dog with jowly cheeks. It could be Old Mother Hubbard's dog, or a dog from another nursery rhyme. It could also be a bear. It's all in how it is drawn.

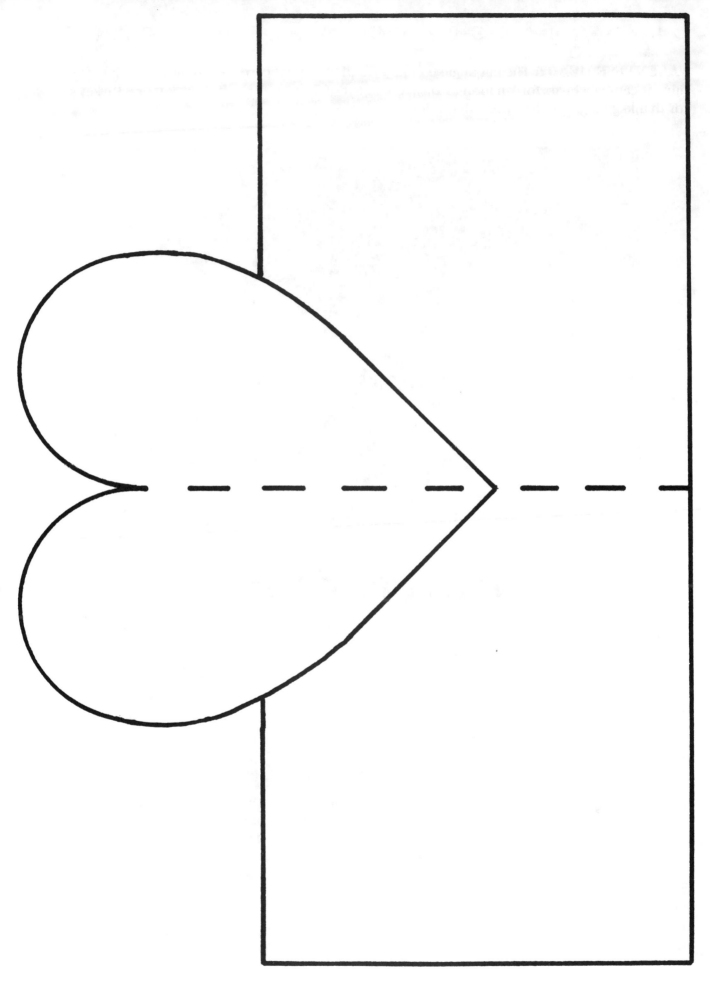

PLEAT BOOKS

Pleats are fun. Perhaps you made these accordion style paper figures when you were in school. They can be any figure you like. Below are directions for snowpeople. But with imagination, the pleats could be ghosts, little houses for a village, or even bunnies.

It's easy to get carried away and want to make six folds in the pleat. However, you will find that, with six figures, the pleats don't fold properly when the book is closed, and they stop working. What you can do is glue down two figures on both sides.

Snowman/Snowwoman

MATERIALS: tag board, heavy construction paper, scissors, crayons, glue

DIRECTIONS:

1 - Cut a piece of white construction paper in half horizontally creating two pieces 6 by 12 inches long.

2 - Take one piece of 6-by-12-inch paper and fold it in half. Crease well.

3 - Open the paper. Using the center crease as a guide, fold the paper accordion style into four sections.

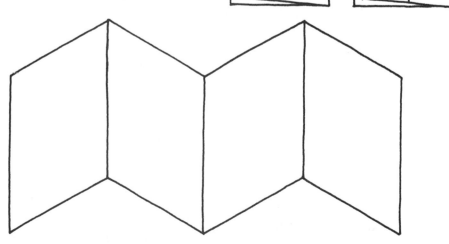

4 - Keep the section folded, draw snowman/snowwoman on the first fold. Be sure the bottom circles of the snowman touch well at the edges. This is what keeps the pleat together and gives it stability.

5 - Cut out the snowpeople. Do not cut along the side edges of the bottom circle of the snowman/snowwoman. Open the pleat to reveal four snowpeople.

6 - Each snowman/snowwoman can be decorated individually, using crayons and construction paper.

7 - After finishing the decorating, fold a piece of tag board in half and color the background scene.

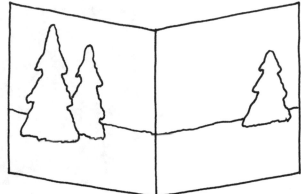

8 - Fold the snowpeople back into a fan and put glue on the back of the first and last figures.

9 - Visually align the crease between the middle two snowpeople with the center crease of the tag board. Place outer snowperson about 3/4 of an inch from either edge of tag board. The center two snowpeople will stand up from the page.

Literature

The Snowman by Raymond Briggs

The Black Snowman by Phil Mendez

WHEEL BOOK

Template on page 105

Wheels are especially good for sequential events as in the growth of a bean into a plant or the change of seasons. Wheels also work well when there are many of the same type of creature on the move as in ants going into an ant hill or the rats of Hamelin following the Pied Piper. The wheel can also be used to give the illusion of movement, as in balls being tossed overhead by a juggler or clouds moving in a storm.

The basic directions for the wheel are the same, regardless of what you decide to draw. There is a sample window with the wheel template. You can vary the size and shape of the window, however, to best suit your project.

MATERIALS: tag board, compass, utility knife, brads, crayons, felt-tip markers or colored pencils

1 - Fold one piece of tag board in half. On another piece of tag board use the compass to draw a circle with a 5 1/2 inch diameter. Mark the center with a dot.

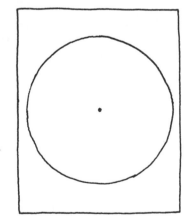

2 - Cut out the circle. Hold in behind the right side of the tag board so that the edge of the circle protrudes slightly from the edge of the page.

3 - Holding the wheel in place, lift it up to a light to see the dot in the center through the tag board page. Mark it on the tag board.

4 - Decide how large and where the window will be. This depends on what you plan to achieve. A juggler could have a large window so several balls could be seen. However, an ant hill could have a rather small window showing where the ants enter the colony. In either case the window needs to start a quarter inch above the dot and extend no high than 2 inches in any direction from the dot.

5 - Cut out the window with a utility knife.

6 - Place a brad through the dot on the tag board and through the wheel and finish drawing. If you find it difficult to draw on the wheel while it is attached to the tag board, lightly trace the boundaries of the window while it is attached to the tag board and then remove it and finish the drawing. This way, you will know exactly where to draw.

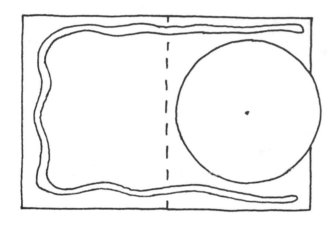

7 - If used by itself, a construction paper cover completes the project. Fold construction paper in half and apply glue around the edges of the tag board but stay clear of the wheel or it will not turn. Use the other side of the page for the written work.

If the wheel is part of a larger book use back-to-back construction to attach the pages.

Ideas and Options

- ○ Excellent for reports, as the left side of the page can be used for the written work.
- ○ Two wheels done on both sides of the page can be used for matching items that go together, such as an animal and its tracks, two things that are red, a math equation and its answer.
- ○ Need more ideas for wheels? How about these: daydreams, a person diving into a pool, an egg hatching, a fish jumping, a television screen, the growth of a frog.

Literature and Content Area Tie-ins

Science— Ant colonies, plant life (the growth of a bean), weather (changing weather, types of clouds, lightning bolts striking), the seasons, ocean life (an octopus, the wheel being the legs of the ocean creature).

Multicultural studies— Make the wheel a spider with moving legs and use it with African tales.

Anansi the Spider: A Tale from the Ashanti by Gerald McDermott.

The Hat Shaking Dance and Other Tales from the Gold Coast by Harold Courlander.

Fables, Nursery Rhymes and Fairy Tales— Make the wheel a spider with moving legs.

(Little Miss Muffett) *The Real Mother Goose*, illustrated by Blanche F. Wright

The Helen Oxenbury Nursery Story Book

The Piped Piper of Hamelin retold by Michele Lemieux

The Piped Piper of Hamelin retold by Mercer Mayer

Holidays— Spider for a Halloween card or story.

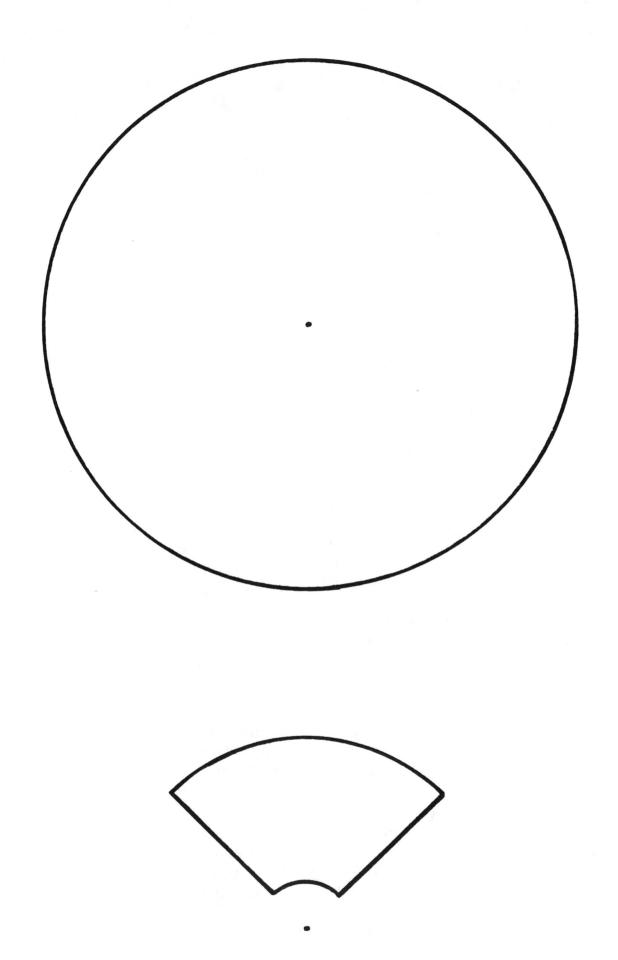

SPLIT CONSTRUCTION BOOKS

This is an interesting design made by cutting, from tag board, a number of pages into a shape and then cutting a slit so they slide together forming a book. If you keep the bottom level, these books stand by themselves.

One of the nicest features of this technique is that you can make it into so many different books. The requirements are simple: the basic shape must be a recognizable subject and it must have a substantial middle section.

The example that follows gives step-by-step directions for a circle. Templates, however, are included for three different split construction shapes: the circle, flowers in a pot, and a turkey. The only difference in construction would be in Step 5. For shapes other than the circle, cut from the top center of the design down on half the shapes and from the bottom center up on the other half. This is necessary for the pages to slip together. Use your imagination and curricular needs to create any different templates you wish: a rabbit, for example, or a butterfly, or a geometric shape.

Literature and Content Area Tie-ins

Triangle— Using a triangular shape, the book can be made to look like a mountain. If the students are writing a report on a particular mountain range or on volcanoes, having many of the same book might actually bring the mountain range to the class. And, if you cut off the top of a mountain, it could be a volcano!

Mountains and Volcanoes by Eileen Curran

Volcanoes of the United States by Ellen Thro

Volcanoes by Franklyn M. Branley

The Mountains of Tibet by Mordicai Gerstein

○ With minimum redesigning, the triangle can also be made into an evergreen tree and a lot of individually made evergreens could be a forest!

○ The inside pages of these books can include illustrations of what might be inside. For example, with the tree above, the students might show the birds and other animals that live in the tree as one of the illustrations. Another possibility would be to show the inside of the trunk where squirrels or a raccoon might be cuddled up.

Flowers in a Pot—- This makes a nice gift book done in bright and happy colors and could be used for many occasions from a get well card to a gift book for spring celebrations.

Turkey— The turkey is perfect for Thanksgiving stories.

Turkeys, Pilgrims and Indian Corn: The Story of the Thanksgiving Symbols by Edna Barth.

Fried Feathers for Thanksgiving by James Stevenson

The First Thanksgiving Feast by Joan Anderson

How Many Days to America? A Thanksgiving Story by Eve Bunting

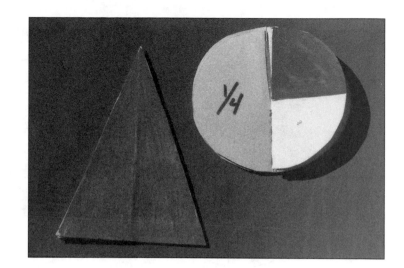

Circle

Adapt for flowers in a pot, butterfly, and turkey—templates on pages 109–112.

MATERIALS: tag board, compass, scissors, cloth tape and crayons

DIRECTIONS:

1 - Using a compass, draw five identical circles. In the template the circles have a 4-inch diameter. However, they can be as large as suits your project.

2 - Cut out all circles.

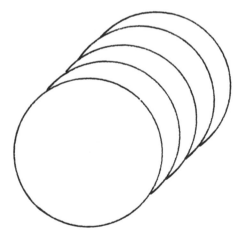

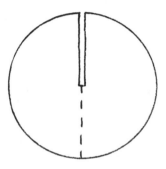

3 - Fold circles in half, creasing well.

4 - Set one circle aside.

5 - Along the crease, cut 2 1/4 inches into the circles. To determine how far to cut on larger circles, simply divide the diameter in half and add a quarter of an inch. For any other split construction book, remember to cut half of the page up from the bottom and the other half down from the top so that the pages slip together forming the book.

6 - To connect the circles, slide one of the circles onto the other three along the slit. See illustration.

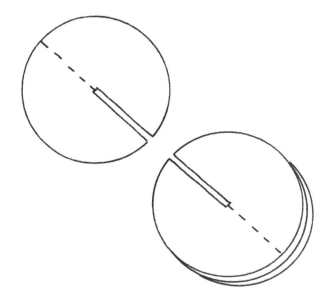

7 - Tape the inside page along the length of the center to improve stability and glue to circle you set aside.

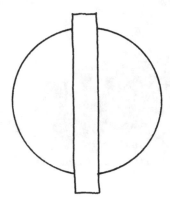

8 - If added stability is necessary, tape along the crease of the last page as well. Usually, this is not necessary.

9 - Complete drawing of cover.

10 - Fanned out, the book looks like this.

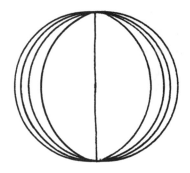

Literature and Content Area Tie-ins

Circle— Math, the study of fractions and symmetry.

Nutrition/Food Groups— The book can be a page of plates onto which the students draw a favorite meal, a well-balanced breakfast, lunch and supper.

Sports— The book can be shaped into a baseball, soccer ball or basketball.

Summer Fun— The book can be a beach ball.

Holiday— Make the book an ornament and read with *Christmas Tree Memories* by Aliki.

Ecology— If made as an Earth, the book could be about ecology or environmental studies.

Mapping— If made as a globe, the book could be about maps and navigation.

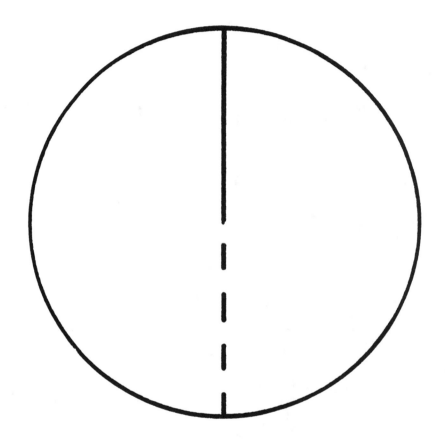

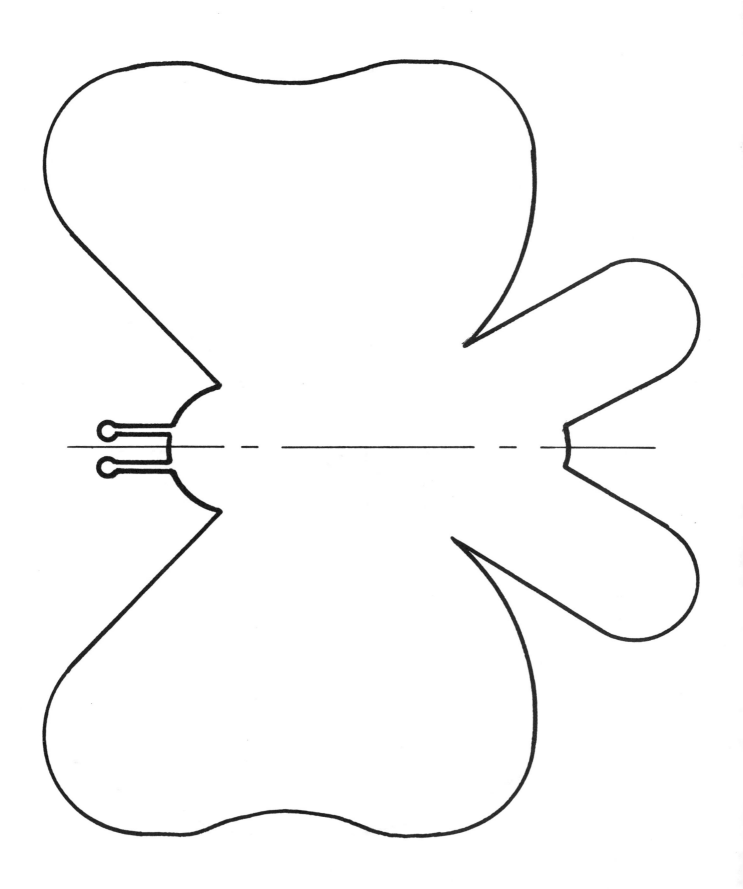

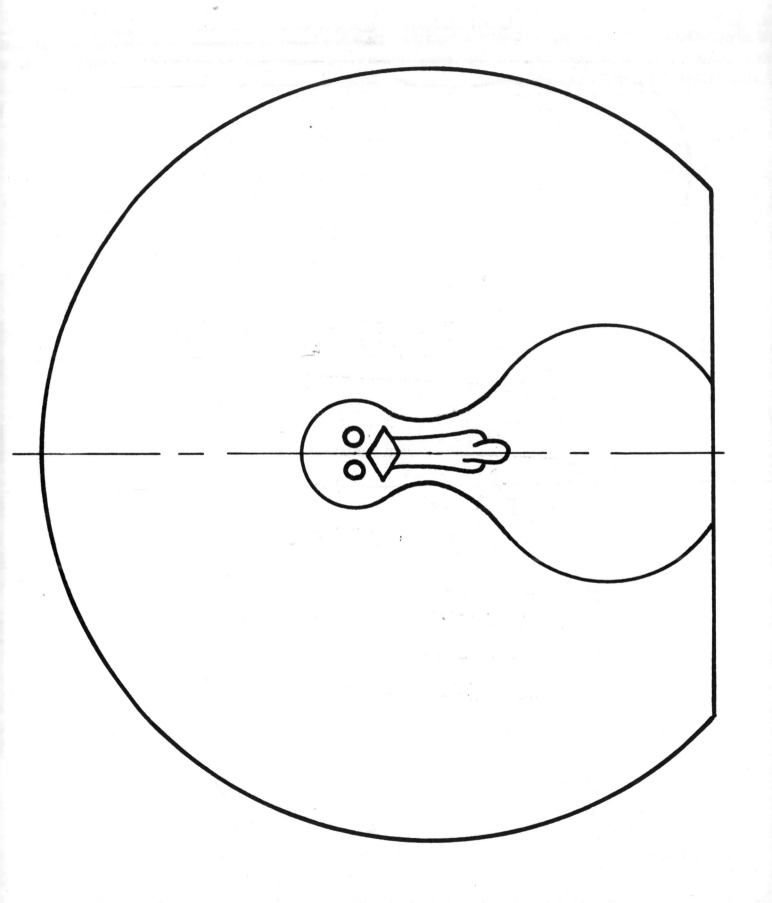